JOSHUA

A SELF-STUDY GUIDE

Irving L. Jensen

MOODY PRESS

CHICAGO

Contents

Introduction

The main purpose of this study guide is not to make Bible study easier but to make it more interesting and fruitful. Many helps are given in each lesson to aid your study, but these are offered to encourage independent searching for the gems in the Scriptures.

Incorporated in this guide are various helps on analyzing the Bible chapter by chapter and paragraph by paragraph. Convinced that "the pencil is one of the best eyes," I have also given suggestions on how the student may record his analyses on paper.

If you are in earnest that your personal Bible study be fruitful, you will appreciate the significance of the following four words:

1. THIRST: The soul should continually thirst for a deeper understanding of the Word of the Lord. Desire is the first key to fruitful Bible study.

2. TOIL: More blessing in Bible study will come if we work as hard in it as we do in other pursuits of life. A servant of God should be a good worker.

3. TIME: There is no shortcut to effective Bible study. We must take the time to tarry long over the precious Book.

4. TEACHABLENESS: We do not come to the Bible to do something to it but to let it do something to us. And the productive measure of such a work will be in proportion to our submission to the Holy Spirit as our Teacher.

As you begin your study of the book of Joshua, determine to be a good Bible student. Let these four T's be continual reminders to you.

Suggestions Directed Especially to Teachers

1. If any lesson seems too long for one meeting, study half the assigned work and leave the other half for the next meeting. Assign no more than the class can study thoroughly.

2. If possible, make enlarged copies (either on cloth or paper) of the maps and charts appearing in this book for teaching aids. Because much geography is involved in the study of Joshua you should thoroughly acquaint your class with the topography of Palestine, pointing out the important sites in each lesson.

3. Insist that the members of the class study the lesson at home and bring their written assignments to class. Urge them to closely follow the order of study given in each lesson. The "Comments" sections should never be read until after the student has finished his own study.

4. Briefly review the previous work at the beginning of each meeting.

5. Insist that the members of the class think and study for themselves. A discussion in which they can express their thoughts and ask questions is preferable to a lecture.

6. Emphasize the importance of carefully looking up all the Scripture references given in each lesson.

7. If you are studying the Bible book by book, you have probably already studied Genesis, Exodus, Leviticus, Numbers, and Deuteronomy. These five books record in order the origin, sin, redemption, and discipline of Israel, and bring the nation to the border of their inheritance, ready to enter into the fullness of all that God promised them (which is the story of Joshua).

8. Unless otherwise stated, all Bible quotations in this study guide are from the King James Version. It is recommended that you consult other versions (e.g., Berkeley) for clarification when necessary.

Lesson 1
Background and Survey

The book of Joshua picks up the history of Israel from the point where Deuteronomy ended. Moses had led the nation up to the border of their promised inheritance and had given them his final counsel, exhortation, and blessing. Then, after being allowed to gaze upon the land of promise, he passed from earth to be with God.

Moses' lifework was done, but Israel's was not. They had to cross the Jordan, drive out the enemy, and possess the land. Under the leadership of Joshua they successfully carried out the mandate.

I. BACKGROUND

At the outset it will be helpful to acquaint yourself with the background of Joshua. This kind of familiarity always enhances personal Bible study.

A. Author and Date

The author of the book of Joshua is not explicitly identified. But the general tenor of the book indicates that he was an eyewitness of most of the events, which are described with great vividness and minuteness of detail, and occasionally in first person ("we" and "us"; e.g., 5:6). The unity of style in the organization of the book indicates that one author wrote the bulk of the work.

In all probability the book was written by Joshua himself, with a few additions (e.g., reference to Joshua's death, 24:29-28) made by other writers, possibly Eleazar or his son Phinehas. Jewish tradition uniformly attributes the book to Joshua.

The book was written not long after the events themselves had transpired. If the conquest of Canaan was completed around

GEOGRAPHY OF THE BOOK OF JOSHUA
Showing the three major campaigns and land allotments

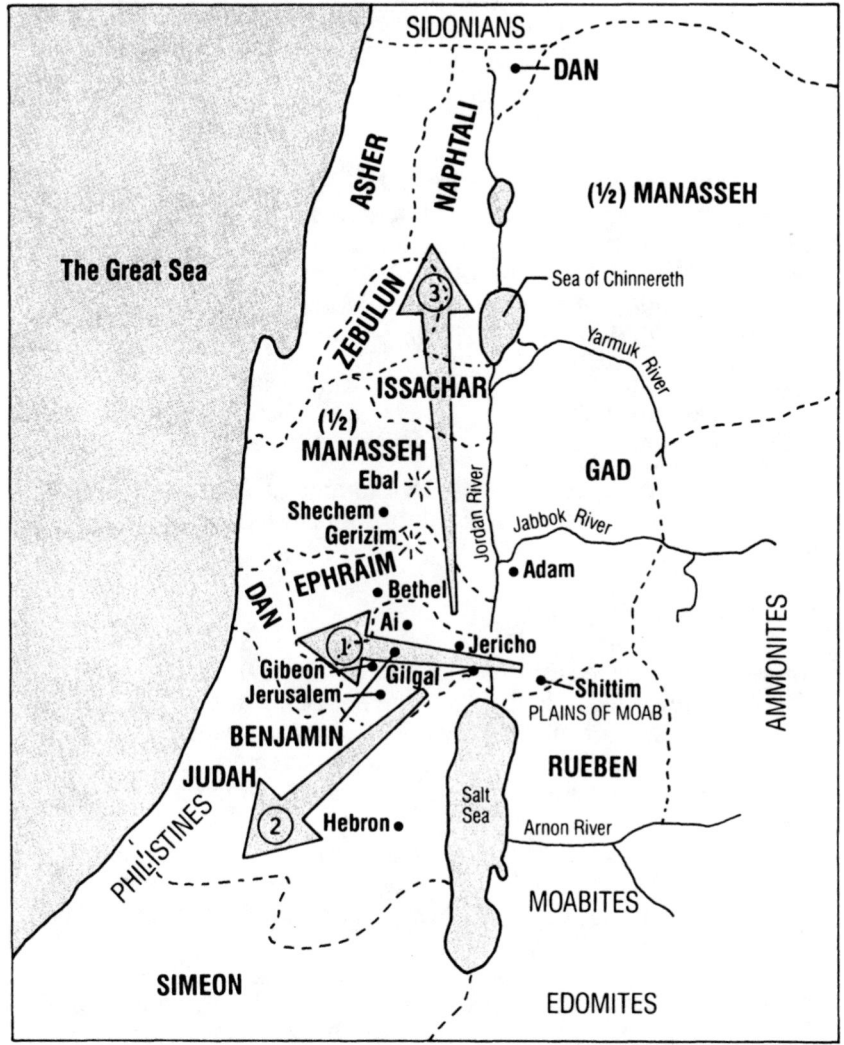

1400 B.C., the book was written soon after this. (Note: Concerning dates of this period of Old Testament history, see John C. Whitcomb's excellent chronological chart *Old Testament Patriarchs and Judges.*)

Some twenty-four years are covered by the narrative of Joshua. After the Canaanites were conquered, Joshua divided the land, settled the tribes in their respective places, and looked after the affairs of the nation until his death.

B. Place in the Bible

In our Bible, Joshua, the sixth book, is the first of the historical books. In the Jewish Old Testament it is the first book of the prophets, probably so classified because its historical record illustrates the basic truths that the prophets preached.

The relation of Joshua to the two books preceding it (in the order of our Old Testament) is simple:

Numbers:	Journey to Canaan
Deuteronomy:	Preparation to enter Canaan
Joshua:	Conquest of Canaan

Study the contents of the books that immediately follow Joshua in the Old Testament canon to further confirm its logical placement in the list.

C. Style and Message

This book is the history of a military campaign. If Moses was a shepherd-leader, surely Joshua was a general-leader, to be classed in the front rank of military commanders along with Caesar, Hannibal, and Napoleon. He was one of the greatest strategists that ever lived, but we must remember that his wisdom came from God.

Joshua is the account of one long triumph. It took seven years to conquer the land of Canaan, but in those seven years Joshua lost only one major battle. His secret of success was implicit faith and absolute obedience to God.

Joshua might be called the Book of Conquest. For those Christians who would be "overcomers" in the "good fight of faith" (1 Tim. 6:12), the book will be most profitable, because it illustrates how a Christian may overcome his spiritual foes and possess what God has for him in Christ. The book is full of encouragement for the spiritual soldier. Those who are satisfied to be "wilderness" Christians, simply saved from the *penalty* of sin, will miss the richest blessings of Joshua. But those determined to be saved also from the *power* of sin, to reign with Christ and be soldiers of the cross, will receive much strength and encouragement from this book.

D. Symbols and Types

Throughout your study of Joshua you will want to identify the major symbolical teachings in the narrative. Only a few of the outstanding ones are mentioned here.

First, review the major typical lessons of the books immediately preceding Joshua. (As stated earlier, the book of Joshua will be more meaningful to one who has already studied the books of the Pentateuch.) There is a remarkable correspondence between the experiences of Israel, from the bondage of Egypt to the conquest of Canaan, and the spiritual experiences of the individual soul. In Exodus we read of (1) Israel's condition in Egypt (bondage, poverty, imminent death), corresponding to the spiritual condition of a soul before regeneration; and (2) Israel's exodus from Egypt, typifying God's deliverance of a soul, bringing salvation. In Numbers we read of Israel's condition in the wilderness (unbelief, disobedience, discontent, weakness), picturing a soul regenerated but not fully yielded to God.

The close of Joshua shows the commencement of Israel's life in Canaan to be one of peace, joy, wealth, power, and victory, typifying a saved soul wholly surrendered to God.

Three prominent types in Joshua are:

1. Joshua, leader of the host of Israel, is a type of Christ, the "captain of our salvation." (Read Heb. 2:10-11; Rom. 8:37; 2 Cor. 1:10; 2:14.)

2. The crossing of the Jordan is a type of the Christian's dying with Christ. (Read Rom. 6:6-11; Eph. 2:5-6; Col. 3:1-3.)

3. Israel's conquest of Canaan typifies the Christian's victories over the enemies of his soul.

As you proceed in your study of Joshua, be sure to keep these major types in mind.

E. The Man Joshua

After you have finished studying the book of Joshua, you will feel that you have come to know this man of God intimately. At this point a few general identifications are sufficient:

1. *His name.* Joshua's original name was Hoshea (Num. 13:8; Deut. 32:44), which means literally "salvation." During the wilder-

ness journey Moses changed the name to Jehoshua, meaning "Jehovah is salvation" (Num. 13:16). Joshua is a contracted form of Jehoshua. What is the significance of this change of name?

2. *His association with Moses.* Joshua was a young man when Moses appointed him as one of his ministers, or attendants, during the wilderness journey. Read the following passages that tell of some of his services during those years: Exodus 17:8-16; 24:12-13; Numbers 13:1-16; 14:26-35. At the close of Moses' career God chose Joshua to be his successor (Num. 27:18), and Moses transferred the mantle of leadership to his faithful attendant and friend (Deut. 34:9).

3. *His character.* Read what God said of Joshua in Numbers 27:18 (cf. Deut. 34:9). Joshua feared God, believed God, obeyed God, and glorified God. These and other godly traits appear throughout the book bearing his name.

II. SURVEY

If you have used the study manuals of other books in this series, you are aware of the procedure to be followed in the survey stage. Your main activities should be:

1. First read the book through in one sitting if possible.

2. Jot down on paper your impressions from this first reading (e.g., What is the atmosphere of the book?).

3. Return to the beginning of the book and assign a title to each of the twenty-four chapters. Record them on the horizontal chart. (Note: A segment should begin at 11:16 instead of 12:1.)

4. Before studying the outline on the accompanying chart, try to group the chapters on your own. Look for turning points in the book, and make your own survey chart, if possible.

5. Now study the accompanying survey chart. Observe the following:

(a) Since the task given Joshua was to take the land (cf. 1:6), the theme of the book is conquest.

(b) The first five chapters describe Israel's preparation for the battles to come, and chapters 6 through 12 record the actual battles. At the end of this section a key summary statement reads, "So Joshua took the whole land" (11:23).

(c) Whereas chapters 1-12 mainly record action, the last half of the book is almost devoid of action. The allocations of the inheritances are recorded in chapters 13-21, and the book closes on a warm note of appeal and consecration (chaps. 22-24).

(d) As shown on the chart, the atmosphere of the last section (chaps. 22-24) is the anticipation of dwelling in the land of Canaan, which is the subject of the books following Joshua.

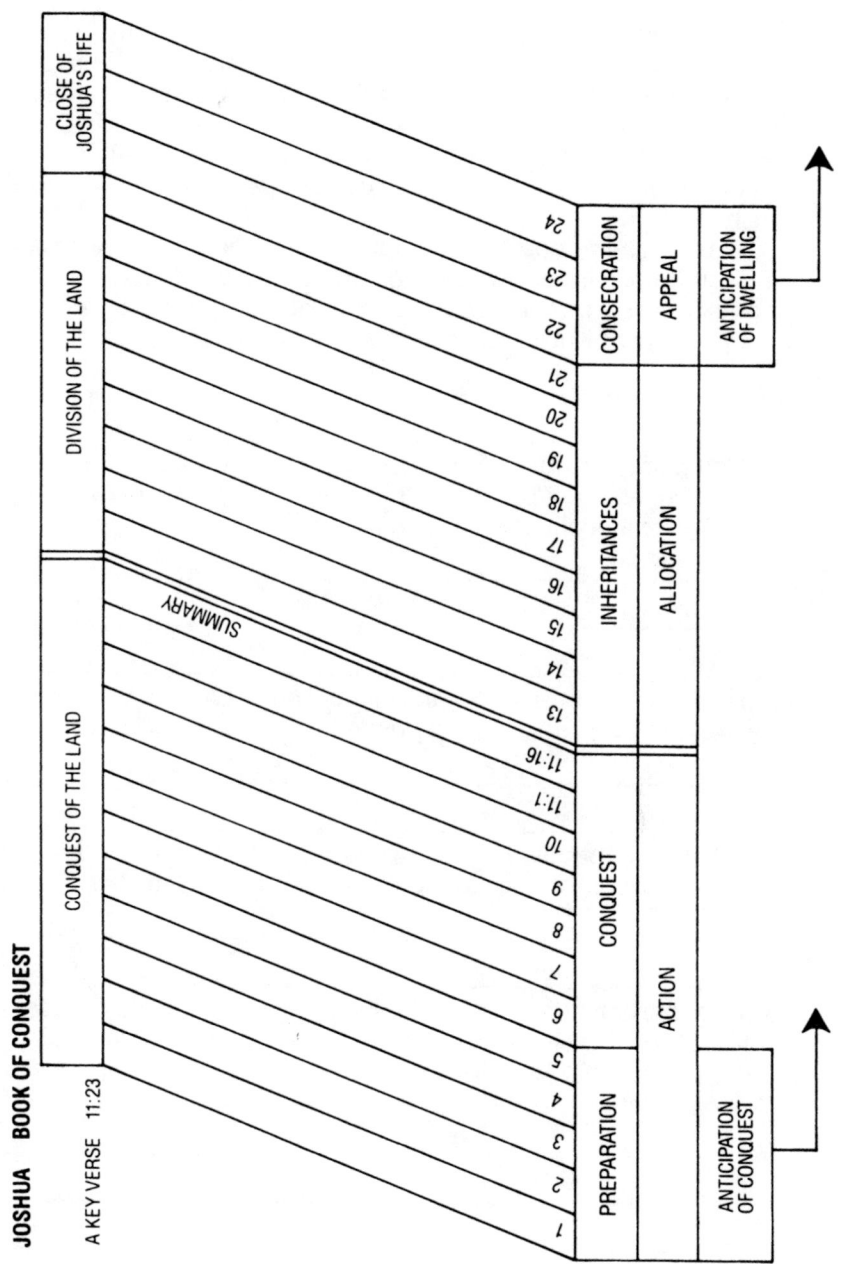

One of the practical purposes of a survey is to discover the outstanding truths of the book. These truths may then be used as guides to observing and interpreting the hosts of individual items that are studied in a more detailed analysis. Beware of failing to see the forest for the trees. From time to time in your study of the individual chapters of Joshua you should review the overall picture.

As a conclusion to this lesson it would be profitable to consider the prominent truths of Joshua and their intended applications. List these truths after you have done the following exercises:

1. In your own words, state the theme of Joshua.

_____

_____

2. God said to Joshua, "Thou shalt cause this people to inherit the land" (1:6, ASV*). What is the relationship between _conquest_ and _inheritance_ in Joshua?

_____

_____

3. The Israelites were _promised_ all the land of Canaan. What determined how much they would _possess_?

_____

4. If faith and obedience were requirements for conquering the land, what were the requirements for holding the land?

_____

5. What important aspect of Christian living is typified by Israel's conquest of Canaan? Read Hebrews 4 and interpret the phrase "entering into God's rest." (Refer to this topic in _Numbers and Deuteronomy_ of this series.)

_____

_____

_____

American Standard Version.

Lesson 2

Joshua 1:1–2:24

Mobilization and Reconnaissance

The first five chapters of Joshua are devoted to preliminary stages of the Israelites' conquest of Canaan, as they prepared and positioned themselves for the battles against their enemies. The first battle, against the city of Jericho, is recorded in chapter 6.

Here is an outline of the main contents of chapters 1-5:

Chapter	EVENT	SIGNIFICANCE
1	Charge to Joshua	Task identified
2	Spying Jericho	Enemy studied
3	Crossing Jordan	Leader magnified
4	Stones set up	Deliverance memorialized
5	Circumcision and Passover	Hearts prepared

Chapter 1: Mobilization

I. ANALYSIS

First read chapter 1 of Joshua a few times, carefully and prayerfully. It is of utmost importance in a Bible study to become thoroughly familiar with the subject matter. No one should ask what a Scripture passage *means* until he knows what it *says*. Underline words and phrases in your Bible that seem especially significant.

Observe that the first nine verses record the Lord's charge to Joshua and Joshua's response, and the last nine verses record Joshua's charges to the Israelites, and their response.

A. Verses 1-9

Let us study verses 1-9 first. Mark in your Bible new paragraphs at verses 3, 5, 7 and 9. Read this segment with those paragraphs in mind, and begin to record some observations on the accompanying chart. Try to determine what each paragraph adds to the account, that is, its uniqueness. This phase of your study will throw much light on the entire passage.

1. See 1:1-2. Show how this paragraph revolves around the two persons Moses and Joshua.

_____

_____

_____

_____

JOSHUA 1:1-9

1
3
5
7
9

Recapitulation

14

2. See 1:3-4 and 1:5-6. Study these two paragraphs together. What is the main subject of each?

_____

_____

3. See 1:7-8. What conditions for success are cited here?

_____

_____

4. See 1:9. How is this a summary of all that goes before? Why does God sometimes repeat words of exhortation and command? What is the value of repetition in teaching?

_____

_____

_____

_____

5. List some important spiritual lessons taught by this segment.

_____

_____

_____

_____

_____

B. Verses 10-18

Now let us concentrate on 1:10-18. Paragraph divisions should be made at verses 12 and 16. You may want to block out a rectangle for this segment, as you did for 1:1-9.
1. (1:10-11) What do you consider the key word or phrase here?

_____

2. (1:12-15) What is the impact of the word "remember" (1:13)? Read Numbers 32:1-42 in this connection. What is the basis of Joshua's appeal?

_____

_____

_____

3. (1:16-18) Analyze the various ingredients of the reply of the two and one-half tribes.

_____

_____

_____

4. What spiritual truths have you learned from these verses?

_____

_____

II. COMMENTS

After Moses' death, God commanded Joshua to take his place at the head of the nation and lead the people over Jordan into the Promised Land. It is enlightening to learn what God chose to include in His eight-verse charge to Joshua, considering the multitude of things He might have said.

Humanly speaking, God set before Joshua an impossible task. How could 2 million people be led across such a river, high and turbulent at that time of the year, when enemy nations on the other side of the Jordan were expected to prevent such an invasion?

Look at the map on page 18 and read the names of the great nations that then inhabited Canaan. These nations were well versed in war, firmly entrenched in strong walled cities, and prepared to fight for every foot of their territory. (Note: The map shows only the locations where the enemy nations were probably concentrated. Segments of the population were found in other locations as well.)

But in giving such a command, God also spoke words to Joshua intended to dispel all his fears. First God gave a view of the inheritance (1:3-4). Surely those valuable possessions were worth having. But could the enemies that held them be overcome? As if to remove any such fear from Joshua's mind, God gave him next the assurance of success (1:5). He revealed to Joshua what would be the secret of his success—a secret that will insure the success of any child of God anywhere and anytime—constant meditation on the Scriptures and obedience to their commands (1:7-8). With all this, Joshua was given the promise of God's continual presence (1:9).

Thus encouraged, Joshua was not afraid to undertake to lead the people into Canaan, difficult as the task appeared from a merely human standpoint.

When God had finished speaking, Joshua sent an order throughout the camp that must have sent a thrill of rapture through every heart. The promise that their forefathers had forfeited was soon to be fulfilled for them.

If this had been the old unsurrendered crowd of the wilderness, which rebelled against every command given them, they would no doubt have objected to this order to cross the Jordan. They would have begun to murmur and complain, saying, "Why such haste? We've been many years on the way to get this far—why not wait until the river lowers?"

But this was not the old wilderness crowd. Under the influence of Moses' farewell address the nation had evidently seen the futility of trusting in their own strength, wisdom, and judgment and had resolved to put themselves unreservedly under God's direction. (See Deut. 34:9.) They surrendered absolutely and unconditionally to God, and in the power of their faith they sent back this answer to their leader: "All that thou commandest us we will do, and whithersoever thou sendest us, we will go" (1:16). This was the company that God led on to victory, enabling them to take Canaan in seven years. We too will experience victorious living if we present ourselves wholeheartedly to our great Joshua—Jesus —with the same words, "Whatsoever Thou commandest us we will do, and whithersoever Thou sendest us we will go."

* * *

Chapter 2: Reconnaissance

Before analyzing the text, study a topographical map of the general area referred to in these chapters. Form such a map try to visualize the physical factors that had to be taken into account in

ENEMY NATIONS CONQUERED BY JOSHUA

Showing the approximate locations of the seven nations (in bold letters) cited in Deuteronomy 7:1 and Joshua 24:11

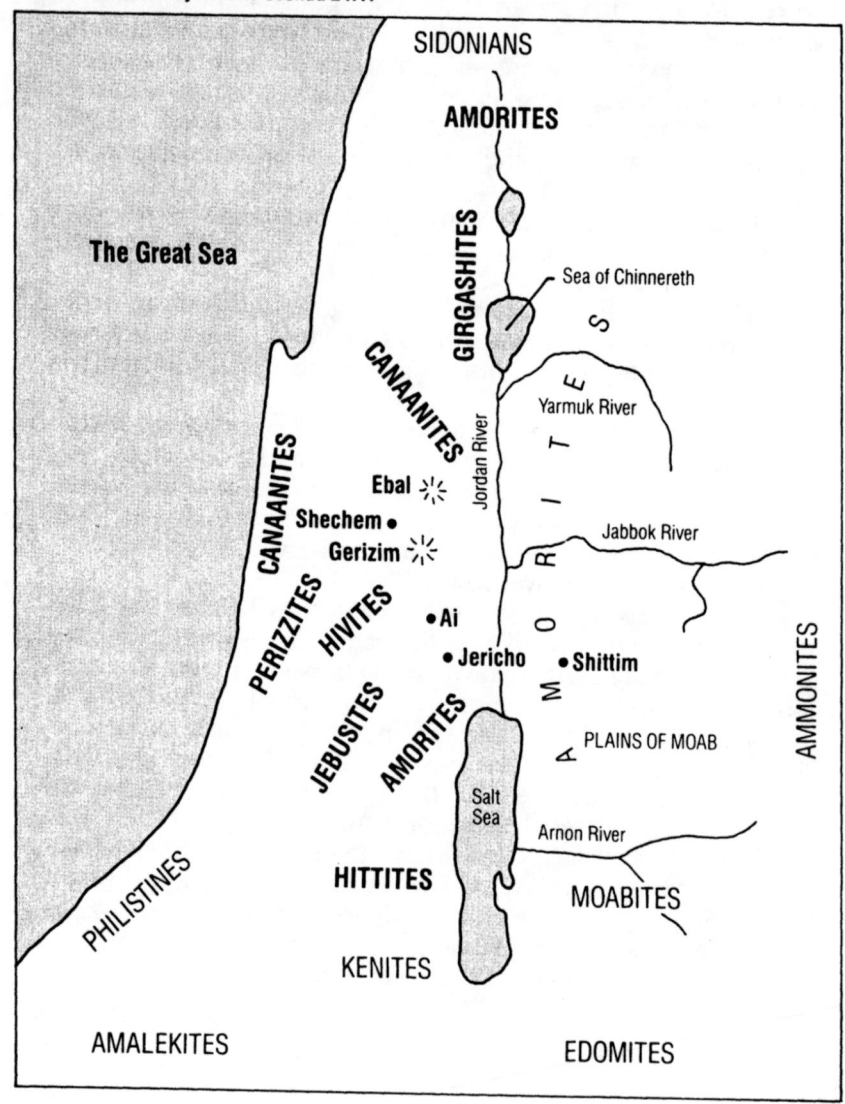

planning a strategy of occupation of Canaan from the starting point of the plains of Moab on the eastern side of the Jordan. Why would the taking of the stronghold of Jericho be a key to the initial stages of such a campaign?

I. ANALYSIS

Proceed with your study, following the suggestions given earlier in this lesson. For this chapter, recognize paragraph divisions at verses 2, 8, 15, and 22.

The spies and Rahab are the main persons in this narrative. Write below the parts played by these people in each of the paragraphs:

Chapters	SPIES	RAHAB
1		
2-7		
8-14		
15-21		
22-24		

On the basis of your study, answer the following:

1. Was Joshua displaying lack of faith by dispatching spies? If not, account for such an assignment.

_____

_____

2. In which paragraph is recorded the valuable information that the spies wanted to obtain? What was that information?

_____

_____

3. What may be learned from the unusual circumstance that it was a harlot, through a lie, who helped the spies? (Study Ex. 15:13-18;

James 2:25; Heb. 11:31; Matt. 1:5). Could God have protected the spies without Rahab's lie?

_____

_____

4. What was Rahab's personal testimony regarding God?

_____

5. What acts of God had impressed the Canaanites?

_____

6. What are some of the major spiritual lessons of chapter 2?

_____

_____

_____

II. COMMENTS

Let us review some of the highlights of the story. While preparations were being made in the camp for crossing the Jordan, Joshua sent two men over the river to spy secretly and "view the land, even Jericho." Jericho would be the first city to resist Israel's advance once they crossed the river, and it was well to measure her strength, look facts in the face, and know what sort of foe they must meet.

Whenever some formidable obstacle stands in the way of our spiritual progress it is well to give it a long straight look, recognizing its power, and then turn our eyes upward to our God, who is infinitely stronger than all our foes, however threatening.

The presence of the two men in Jericho was quickly discovered, and the king sent to Rahab, in whose house they were lodging, a command to surrender the spies. But Rahab hid them on the housetop and told the king's messengers that although the men of Israel had been in her house, they had left while it was dark.

With no suspicion that Rahab was playing them false, the messengers were off. Then the woman went up on the housetop to make an agreement with the men whose lives she had saved. She revealed to them that terror had fallen upon the inhabitants of Canaan because of the Israelites; that when they heard of the wonders that God had wrought for His people, and of their great victories on the east of Jordan, the hearts of the inhabitants melted, and their courage failed. She expressed her belief that the Lord their God was the true God and that He would give them the land of Canaan. Then she asked that when they came to take possession they would spare her life and the lives of her kindred. To this the spies agreed, on the conditions that she gather her relatives into her house, identify her dwelling by the scarlet cord in the window, and would not utter their business in Jericho.

When Sodom was to be destroyed, God sent His angels and brought Lot out. Now God was about to destroy Jericho, but He would save Rahab, who had faith in Him.

From the story of Rahab many lessons may be learned, two of which are cited here:

1. God saves, not because of one's righteousness, but because of one's faith.

It might be asked, was not Rahab a sinful woman? Yes. Did she not lie to the king of Jericho? Yes. How then could she be saved? She was saved by faith, not by her own righteousness. God saved her not because she was good but that she might become so.

It is not to be supposed from Hebrews 11:31 and James 2:25 that God commended Rahab's falsehood or any of her other sins. These passages point out her living faith, which was manifested by her works that followed.

In the same way the thief on the cross was saved by faith, and he abundantly proved the reality of his faith by his works that followed, namely: confession of his own guilt, public confession of faith in Christ's power to save, his fear of God, his rebuking of sin, his calling upon Christ to remember him, all seen in his few words as he hung on the cross. (See Luke 23:39-43.)

2. God has rich rewards for those who believe and obey Him.

Read Joshua 6:25 and Matthew 1:5 to learn how Rahab's ensuing years were blessed of God. When her life was spared she joined the people of God and dwelt among them. Later on she married one of the men of Judah and became an ancestress of the Lord Jesus Christ.

How exceeding abundantly God wrought for her above all that she asked or thought. He saved her from death, placed her among His children, enlightened and instructed her, brought her into the royal line, and gave her a part in Christ. So will He do for any sinner, however ignorant or degraded or far from God, if he will only believe and obey.

Before leaving this second chapter, study again the report that the two spies brought back to Joshua (vv. 23 and 24). This report is quite different from that which the ten spies brought back forty years earlier to Moses at Kadesh-barnea. This has the ring of faith and sounds like the words of the report of Joshua and Caleb to Moses. (See Num. 14:6-9.) It contains no note of discouragement or fear and must have given the people fresh courage and resolve.

III. SUMMARY

When God gave the charge to Joshua after Moses' death, it was to identify his life's task (chap.1). When Joshua sent two spies to Jericho in anticipation of entering Canaan, it was to study the enemy (chap. 2). In both experiences Joshua was assured of deliverance. God promised: "There shall not any man be able to stand before thee.... I will be with thee" (1:5). Through the reconnaissance, the spies foresaw deliverance. "Truly the Lord hath delivered into our hands all the land" (2:24).

Lesson 3

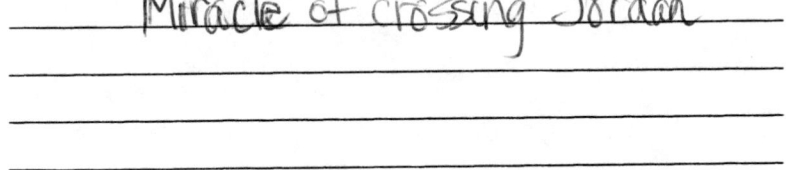

Crossing the Jordan

Joshua and the two spies were convinced that God would give His people victory in battles to come. But how were they to share this assurance with 2 million people? Actually, God took the initiative to demonstrate in a miraculous way that it would be by *His* might, not by the mere might of Israel's armies, that deliverance would come. This was one of the reasons for the miracle of the Jordan crossing.

I. ANALYSIS

Before analyzing this section, consult a map showing the following places: Shittim, Adam, Gilgal, Jericho. As you read the story of these chapters, keep vividly before you the geography involved.

Read through the two chapters slowly and carefully. Underline in your Bible key words and phrases.

It will be of great help to you to see what each paragraph contributes to the whole narrative. Record on the accompanying chart, at the place designated, the main point of each paragraph.

Now that you have identified the main point of each paragraph, do the following, recording your study:

1. Identify the subject of each of the three *groups* of paragraphs.

Miracle of crossing Jordan

_____

_____

_____

Intimidating the enemy

	3:1	7	14 17	4:1	8	15	19	5:1
MAIN CONTENT of each PARAGRAPH								
3 GROUPS of PARAGRAPHS	①			②		③		
MAIN CHARACTERS								
references to PURPOSES, REACTIONS, etc.	Joshua became revered leader God was in charge Strengthening faith				Leaving – Entering land promised			

2. Who are the main characters or groups of people in the different parts?

Joshua

Warriors
Trans Jordan tribes

3. Observe throughout the narrative any references to the divine purposes for this miraculous crossing, and reactions by people. This should be one of the most important parts of your study, because some prominent spiritual lessons are derived from it.

Trust the Lord
showing the enemies that God was
in charge

Here are some further questions to be answered now:

1. What were some of the major human or physical problems involved in Israel's crossing of the Jordan? (There were even more problems than those implied by the text.)

people could not swim — flood season
families, herds, possessions

2. What lesson is taught by the people's following the Ark of the Covenant (3:3-4, 11)? Following the priests (3:3, 13)?

Ark represents Jesus
obedience

3. Why were the people commanded to sanctify themselves? (3:5). What do you suppose was involved here?

needed to prepare themselves — confession
washing — abstain from sex, clean clothes + bodies

4. What verse later on in the story refers to the fulfillment of 3:7?

3:16, 4:14

5. More than one miracle was involved in the story of the Jordan crossing. See how many you can identify.

Stopping river, no fear to cross, Canaanites were fearful, water flowed again, priests could hold ark

6. Where were the first twelve memorial stones set up? (4:3, 20). Where were the other twelve stones set up? What was the purpose of memorial stones? Are Christians today served by any kinds of memorials? If so, what are they?

place where you stay tonight
at Gilgal
at the spot where the priests stood in the river

7. In your own words list the chronological sequence of events of this story.

8. What evidence is furnished by 5:1 that the Jordan crossing was miraculous?

enemy believed God dried up the river

9. What do these chapters teach about leadership? About following?

Leadership must be given

10. List other major spiritual lessons to be learned here. (The application of Scripture is, of course, the ultimate purpose of all Bible study.)

Trusted God with their life with obedience — need action

II. COMMENTS

This story took place toward the end of the rainy season, when the Jordan overflowed its riverbanks. Early on an appointed morning Joshua arose and led the people to the brink of the river. As they gazed upon that foaming, swollen stream, they must have wondered how they could ever cross with all their women and children and flocks and herds and household goods.

As Israel lodged there on the brink of the river, preparatory to crossing, officers were sent throughout the camp with clear instructions for the people. The order was to keep their eye on the Ark and follow their leader. If ever they needed to follow, it was now. The seething, foaming waters surely looked like a river of death. The Israelites had not gone that way before, but there was no cause for alarm, because the promise was "The ark of the covenant of the Lord of all the earth passeth over before you into Jordan" (3:11). The Ark of the Covenant, which speaks typically of Christ, was to go before them, and in Jordan it was to stand firmly, its presence staying the mad waters and allowing the Israelites to pass over safely.

God never sends His people out, but that He treads the pathway first. Where the Ark of the Covenant of the Lord is, the waters of death can never overflow.

On the morrow the people saw and experienced the great miracle. First went the little company of priests, dressed in white, bearing on their shoulders the sacred Ark of God. Following at a distance of about three thousand feet came the hosts of Israel by their tribes. As the feet of the priests touched the water, the raging river began to roll backward, piling up in a great wall to their right. And there it stood, until all the people had passed safely over on firm dry ground.

While the priests remained in the middle of the riverbed with the Ark, twelve men were sent back to carry out from the riverbed twelve great stones. These were afterward set up in Gilgal and, together with the twelve stones that Joshua set up in the midst of the river, were to be a memorial of this great event and a constant witness to the mighty power of God.

He who had power to stay those raging waters and bring His people safely over also had power to drive out from before them the Canaanites, the Hittites, the Hivites, the Perizzites, the Girgashites, the Amorites, and the Jebusites. And now Israel was face to face with all these nations. When the priests came up out of the riverbed, the waters returned and flowed over all the banks again. For Israel there was no turning back. They had left the wilderness life forever. They were actually within their promised inheritance, and the next task was to rout the enemies and take possession of the land.

We have already seen that Egypt typifies the world, or Satan's domain, and the wilderness typifies the unsurrendered Christian life, where there is murmuring and wandering, stumbling and failure, disobedience and unbelief. Canaan represents the Spirit-filled life, the absolutely surrendered Christian life, the Christian's position on resurrection ground, where it is no longer self but Christ who rules. It is that life in which one reckons himself as dead and buried with Christ, risen to newness of life in Him and in a position to participate in all the victories and delights of the blessed life in Christ.

Oh, that each child of God might indeed be dead to the appeals of sin and Satan; that when Satan comes—and wants to use his lips, his hands, his feet—he might be dead to Satan's appeals, utterly unresponsive, but alive unto Christ. "Neither yield ye your members as instruments of unrighteousness unto sin; but yield yourselves unto God, as those that are alive from the dead, and your members as instruments of righteousness unto God" (Rom. 6:13).

But it is not to be supposed that when a child of God claims this victorious life, and steps out upon it, he will never have any more conflicts. The Israelites' fiercest battles were in Canaan itself. But in Canaan they were constantly given power to gain the victory.

Gilgal (Hebrew for "circle of stones") was located about ten miles west of the Jordan. It is there that the Israelites first encamped (see map, p. 36). During the war with the people of Canaan this was their headquarters, where the women and children and cattle remained until the land was conquered and divided among the twelve tribes. This, then, was an appropriate place for setting up the memorial stones. As the women and children beheld them, and as the men of war returned again and again from battle, the sight of these stones would call to mind what God had already done for them and what He had promised yet to do.

We too have memorial stones. Every time we partake of the bread and the cup of the Lord's Supper we should look to the cross and see Christ suffering the death that, but for the grace of God, would have overwhelmed us. Then we should look unto the living Christ and thank God for our perfect deliverance. (Read 1 Cor. 11:23-26.) We also have memories of individual experiences, times when God performed the impossible for us. We should let these be good reminders to us of His help in the past. And we should remember that God never changes.

III. SUMMARY

These chapters tell the story of Israel reaching their first objective in Canaan (a camping ground at Gilgal) by crossing over an impassable river. Through the miracle of the crossing God intended to intimidate the enemy, strengthen the faith of the Israelites, magnify Joshua as leader, and glorify His own name by the might of His hand. What God did on that day should remind all people of the earth of how mighty God is.

Lesson 4

Spiritual Renewal

While the enemy kings were dressing their wounds after their setback in morale over the Jordan miracle (5:1), it was time for Joshua and the hosts of Israel to respond to God's provisions and commands for spiritual renewal of their own souls. The Scripture passage for this present lesson is brief, but it contains choice nuggets of truth for the believer. Determine in your analysis of this passage not to overlook any of these nuggets.

As preparation for your analysis, you would do well to first review these three items in Israel's history: circumcision, Passover, and manna.

1. *Circumcision.* Read Genesis 17:1-14 for the record of the first circumcising of the Hebrew males. (Actually, the custom of circumcising was practiced by many of the ancient races of the world, apparently with religious motives.) The Hebrew circumcision was uniquely of divine origin. The rite was instituted by God to be the seal or sign of the covenant that He in grace had made with Abraham. By virtue of this covenant (1) the Lord would be God unto Abraham and his seed; (2) Abraham would be a father of many nations; and (3) Abraham and his seed would be given all the land of Canaan. Circumcision was thus a ratification of this covenant between God and His people. Of course the outward form of circumcision was of no avail if there was not a circumcision of the heart—a pure heart wholly devoted to God (read Deut. 30:6; Lev. 26:41; Ezek. 44:7; Jer. 9:25-26; Rom. 2:29). (Note: For further light on this subject, consult a Bible dictionary.)

2. *Passover.* First read the story of the first Passover—the original event itself—in Exodus 12:1-20. Observe especially the prominment items of the observance. Consider the significance of these phrases:

"It is the Lord's passover" (v. 11)
"Blood shall be to you for token" (v. 13)

"I will pass over you" (v. 13)

"This day shall be unto you for a memorial" (v. 14)

Next read the story of the second observance of the Passover in Numbers 9:1-14. How appropriate was the observance at this time from Israel's standpoint?

For the next forty years the Passover was not observed because the people were not in fellowship with God. The extent of their idolatry during those years is suggested by Amos 5:25-26. Your study of this lesson will reveal that the rite of circumcision was also discontinued during this period. The Passover observance of Joshua 5:10 is the third recorded Passover in the Old Testament.

3. *Manna.* The story of the first provision of this "bread of heaven" (Ps. 105:40) is recorded in Exodus 16:4-36. (After you have read this passage, read the following also: Num. 11:7-9; Deut. 8:3, 16; Ps. 78:24-25; Rev. 2:17.) This manna was miraculous food provided daily by God for Israel during their long wilderness sojourn. The supply ceased as of the day of Israel's experience recorded in Joshua 5.

On the origin of the name"manna," *The Zondervan Pictorial Bible Dictionary* writes, "The name is of uncertain meaning. The Hebrew *man* is a question and added to *hu* would be 'What is it?' On the other hand it may be an adaptation of the Egyptian *mennu,* food. Josephus and other ancient writers attribute the name to the question 'Is it food?' which is in keeping with the wilderness setting."

I. ANALYSIS

Before reading these verses, mark off paragraph divisions in your Bible at verses 2, 10, 11, and 13. Visualize the action of this segment as you read through the passage a few times. Underline the more prominent words and phrases in your Bible. Record some of your observations on paper.

Four prominent symbols or tokens appear in this passage: circumcision, blood, fruit, and sword. One symbol appears in each of the four paragraphs identified by this lesson. Observe how they are recorded on the accompanying chart, and notice what related fact is cited for each. Follow the suggestions for study given below, recording on the chart whenever possible.

1. What other key words appear in the paragraphs? *new life w/God*

2) circumsise again – refers to young men not
3-10) Passover – 1st in the promised land circumcised
11/12) manna – stopped after they ate the produce
13-15) of the land

Commander of the army of the Lord

sword – represented power of God

2. Recall the main significance of each symbol. What was each one teaching Israel, even if by way of recall?

Circumcision – cutting off old – new life w/ God
blood – reminder of their exodus from Egypt &
the mighty miracles of God   fruit – new food – replaced manna

3. Which of the four were new experiences for Israel? Which were old?

circumcision – new for the young generation
passover blood – old
fruit (had in Egypt)   sword – new

4. Study the geography of these paragraphs. The endings of the first and last paragraphs are explicit; what is suggested by the geography of the middle paragraphs?

in Gilgall – stayed there until healed of
circumcision – plains of Jericho

5. Compare the paragraphs in other ways, and record your findings. You will find this an unusually exciting study.

6. Tarry long over the paragraph of verses 13-15. How important was this experience for Joshua at this time? What things do you suppose were going through his mind before he saw the man with the sword? Who was this man? Why was the sword drawn? Who do you think the "host" of verse 14 was? Why the command of verse 15? How significant was this command in view of the next event in Joshua's experience—the conquest of Jericho?

probably fearful, – this encounter
gave him confidence, assurance

Before reading the Comments section of this lesson, write out some of the vital spiritual lessons you have learned from these verses of Joshua.

31

2

SYMBOL: Circumcision—this token spoke mainly of . . .   **COVENANT**

Other key words:
What Israel was reminded of by the symbol:
Old or new?
Reference to place, and its significance:

10

SYMBOL: Blood—this was the main item of the . . .   **PASSOVER**

Other key words:
What Israel was reminded of by the symbol: *reminded of deliverance*
Old or new?
Reference to place, and its significance: *from Egypt*

11

SYMBOL: Fruit—this replaced the temporary . . .   **MANNA**

Other key words:
What Israel was reminded of by the symbol:
Old or new?
Reference to place, and its significance:

13

SYMBOL: Sword—the One who held this was Israel's . . .   **CAPTAIN**

Other key words:
What Israel was reminded of by the symbol:
Old or new?
Reference to place, and its significance:

15

II. COMMENTS

The manna did not cease to fall until the Israelites began to eat of the "old corn of the land" (5:11-12) That was grain standing in the open fields. Such is God's care of His people, that one supply does not fail before another begins.

Just before the first stronghold of Canaan was to be seized, God Himself appeared to Joshua, strengthening and encouraging him (5:13-15). As Joshua stood near Jericho, perhaps thinking of the work ahead of him, "he lifted up his eyes" and beheld Jehovah. Only the uplifted eyes can so behold Jehovah. Joshua did not at first recognize the Man that stood with drawn sword; but when, in answer to Joshua's challenge, "Art thou for us, or for our adversaries?" He said, "Nay, but as captain of the host of the Lord am I now come," Joshua fell on his face and worshiped.

By the fact that Joshua's worship was received, we may conclude that this One who spoke to Joshua was neither man nor angel but the Lord Himself—perhaps the preincarnate Christ, as He appeared more than once before His incarnation.

He told Joshua that He came as Captain of the Lord's host. Who was this host? Recall Christ's words to Peter when the multitude, led by Judas, came to take Him: "Thinkest thou that I cannot now pray to my Father, and He shall presently give me more than twelve legions of angels?" (Matt. 26:53). The words "host of the Lord" did not refer to Israel's army, but to the countless numbers of angelic beings that serve God in guarding and fighting for His servants. (Cf. 1 Kings 22:19; Pss. 103:20-21; 148:2.)

Let us remember that this same One who appeared to Joshua is now Captain of our salvation. In our fierce battles against the principalities, powers, and rulers of this world's darkness—Satan's trained, organized, and fearful hosts—we should look to our Captain, let Him lead on, and know that in His name there is sure and certain victory.

III. SUMMARY

In your own words, summarize this lesson emphasizing the four words:

Circumcision
Blood
Fruit
Sword

Also write out a concluding paragraph showing how each one of these illustrates an important truth about Christian living.

Lesson 5

Conquest of Jericho

Jericho was the first stronghold of the enemy that Joshua was to attack in the war that had been declared by God against the seven condemned nations inhabiting Canaan.

But why had God declared war against the Canaanites? Why had He commanded Israel to "smite them, and utterly destroy them"; to "show no mercy unto them"; to "destroy their name from under heaven" and to "kill everything that breathes"? People criticize God for commanding such annihilation. They have objected, "How cruel to order the death of all those innocent men, women, and children." And they have asked, "Could a God of love order such a thing as that?"

If such opponents of God who dare to criticize Him would read the Bible more closely, they would begin to see some of God's reasons for exterminating the Canaanites. In the first place these nations were desperately wicked. Read in Leviticus 18 the awful list of sins (some of them almost unthinkable), and then read God's statement (Lev. 18:24, 27) that the Canaanites had committed *all those* abominations (also see Deut. 12:31). These people were far from being innocent. They had fallen to such a depth of corruption that God would no longer suffer them to live on the earth. God owns this earth and has a right to eject bad tenants whenever He sees fit. The Canaanites had reached such depths of iniquity that God had to remove them if He would save the human race from corruption such as there was before the Flood. Compare this with the radical surgery performed by the surgeon who must cut out cancer from the quivering flesh in order to save the life and health of the whole body.

Then, too, this land of Canaan belonged to Israel. God, who owns the earth, had deeded this part of it to Abraham and his seed forever (Gen. 12:6-7; 13:14-15, 17). The Canaanites were usurpers.

Moreover, this conflict between Israel and the Canaanites was much more than a struggle of nation against nation. Satan and his hosts had long controlled the inhabitants of that land, and so it was a casting down of Satan as well as a driving out of the nations that was involved. This was truly God's holy war against Satan.

But why did God have *Israel* perform this bloody slaughter? Why did He not destroy these nations by pestilence or famine or in some other way, rather than by war? Perhaps because the Israelites needed the solemn lesson that they learned by being God's executioners. God had warned the Israelites not to learn and practice the abominations of the Canaanites, and it must have been impressed upon their minds and hearts how inviolable was God's

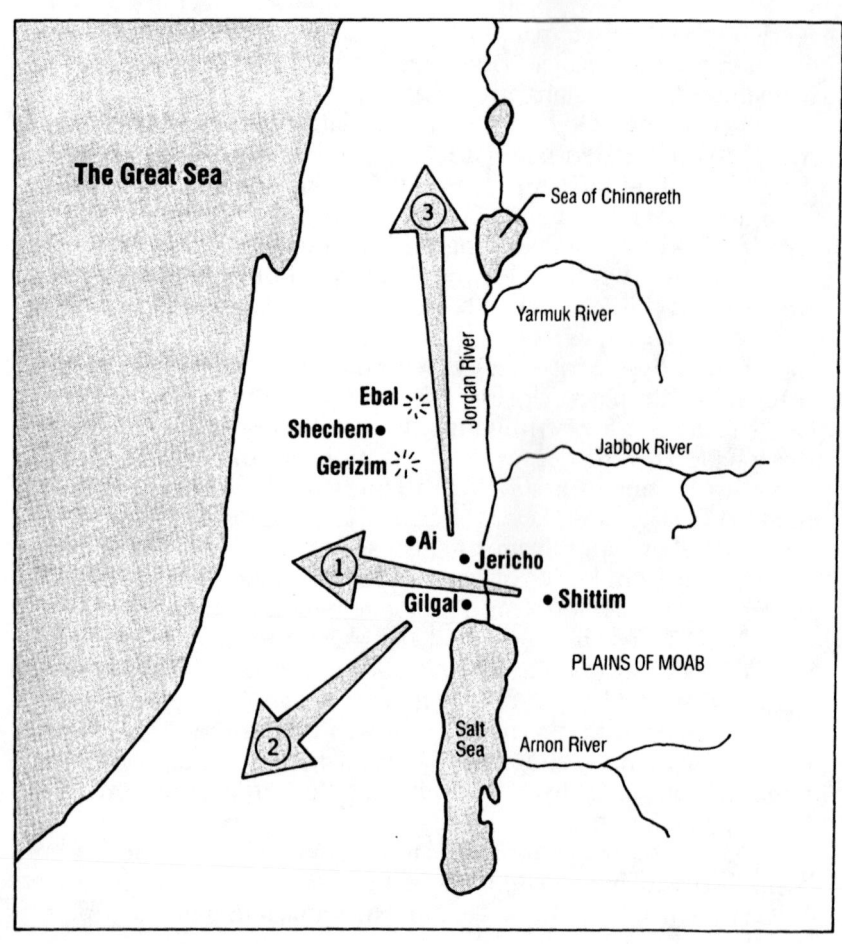

command, as they went about slaying the ones who threatened their souls. For God had also warned Israel that if they as a nation should enter into these abominations and practice these sins, He would drive them also from this land and slay them. (Read Deut. 7:20:16-18.)

I. PREPARATION FOR STUDY

Before studying chapter 6, we should acquaint ourselves with the overall military strategy of Joshua in conquering, and the survey outline of chapters 6-12 which record the military campaigns of Israel.

A. The Three Campaigns

In view of the topography of the land and the distribution of the towns and fortresses of the Canaanites, Joshua's strategy of step-by-step conquest was sound. The accompanying map shows the three general campaigns that Joshua planned. Study the following names and descriptions of the campaigns, and be sure you understand the general strategy of each.

1. The Central Campaign—to secure a bridgehead for the Israelites in the center of the land, from which to spread out.

2. The Southern Campaign—to rout the nearest foes. Many towns and fortresses were located in this area.

3. The Northern Campaign—to gain control of the remaining north territory.

B. Survey of Chapters 6-12

Now let us see how Joshua reported these campaigns in his book. Our interest at this time is only to see the broad outline of his record. Be sure to refer to your Bible as you study the outline, making any notations you may desire.

II. ANALYSIS

First read through the chapter a few times, observing carefully as you read. As part of your first reading include 5:1 for extra background.

In order to see the organization of this chapter more clearly, work with the accompanying chart:

1. Let the observations you record on the chart be starters in your pondering the tremendous truths of this chapter.

CONQUEST JOSHUA 6:1—12:24

JERICHO	AI DEFEATS ISRAEL	ISRAEL DEFEATS AI	ALTAR AT EBAL	PACT WITH GIBEON	5 KINGS SLAIN	OTHER CONQUESTS	NORTHERN CONQUESTS	"So Joshua took all that land"
6:1	7:1	8:1	8:30	9:1	10:1	10:28	11:1	11:16 12:24
CENTRAL CAMPAIGN				SOUTHERN CAMPAIGN			NORTHERN CAMPAIGN	SUMMARY
CRUCIAL BATTLES				PROGRESSIVE CONQUESTS				
SEVEN YEARS								
5	6			7				Lessons of this manual ◀━ here

2. How clear is the Bible in representing Jericho's fall as miraculous? What should the believer's attitude be toward miracles today?

Very, there was no battle no physical reason for the wall to fall

3. What was God teaching the Israelites through the procedures of the seven days leading up to the collapse of the walls? (Do not be content with just one answer; consider various aspects of the procedures.)

obedience, perserverance, patience, trust faith

4. What was the significance of the following:
(a) The positioning of the Ark, the priests, and the armed men?

not military might that would defeat, but God

(b) The many sevens (e.g., vv. 4-5)?

seven is God's perfect number

JOSHUA 6

	1 ASSURANCE AND INSTRUCTIONS 8	MARCHES, AND THE CITY'S FALL	22 DISPOSITIONS AND CURSE 27
Record Main points here→	I have delivered Jericho into your hands ←	march around the city once w/ all armed men for 6 days	Rahab & family are saved
	Joshua ordered people to Advance & March	Marched as ordered by God	Put silver, gold, bronze & iron into the treasury of the Lord's house
References to the Lord	(2) Lord speaks to Joshua	(The Lord has given you the city (accursed) (2) devoted the city to the Lord & destroyed	Curse was on anyone who tried to rebuild the city
Sights & sounds	Jericho shut tightly up	every living thing	The Lord was with Joshua

(c) The silence of verse 10 and the shout of verse 16? Obedience
this was unusual military tactics —

5. In what various ways was the Israelites' *faith* tested here? (Read Heb. 11:30.)

See if they would totally depend on God

6. What were the Israelites forbidden to do upon entering the fallen city? In order to interpret the meaning of "the accursed thing" of 6:18, consider the following: (1) the word translated "accursed" is *herem*, meaning "devoted"; (2) 6:17 speaks of two things "devoted" to the Lord. What were they?   the city & goods

Rahab her family   take the goods from city for themselves

7. What do you learn about God from this chapter?

God expects His instructions to be obeyed
God is faithful, merciful to Rahab

8. How would this experience have prepared Israel for the battles to come?

they were obedient & were successful faith was strengthened

9. Why does the chapter conclude with the salutary verse (27) about Joshua, rather than citing Israel?

Joshua obeyed God, had strong faith — showed him as strong leader

III. COMMENTS

Jericho was the first stronghold that Israel had to conquer in order to possess Canaan. Jericho might be likened to some besetting sin, some habit or practice, which has to be overcome and put away before the richer experiences of the blessed life can be enjoyed. It would never do to pass by a "Jericho" and leave it unconquered. It must be resolutely faced and subdued. But how?

Look at the city: large, strong, surrounded by high, thick walls, guarded by skilled, fierce warriors, stored with abundant supplies to endure a siege, and evidently prepared in every way for such an event (see 6:1).

If the destruction of the city had depended upon Israel, the task would have been hopeless. But it depended upon God. All that Israel had to do was to obey orders. In the second verse of Joshua 6, God said, "I have given into thine hand Jericho." So the victory over this fortress was to be a gift from God, nothing in which Israel could pride themselves.

Now notice carefully how this victory was won, as it will show us how we may gain the victory over some great Jericho in our lives. As Joshua talked with God, the instructions given for the taking of Jericho were made plain, but they involved certainly the most peculiar war strategy that a military leader has ever known. (Read 6:2-5.)

Israel was to form a procession and march around Jericho once a day for six days, and seven times on the seventh day. This procession was to be made up of all the men of war, the Ark of God, and seven priests blowing rams' horns. No word was to be spoken on the march, and no sound heard but the blowing of the horns. But on the seventh day, when they had encompassed the city seven times, they were to shout, and the walls of Jericho would fall down flat.

Suppose Joshua had given these orders to the Israelites of the old wilderness crowd. They would have immediately objected and found fault with the plan. "Whoever heard of such a way to go to war? The idea of taking priests into battle! Fire and scaling ladders would be more useful than horns. What would Moses have thought of such military tactics? Joshua has not a little power now, and is trying to show off!"

Does that not sound like the wilderness crowd, with their faultfinding and criticism, their egotism and disregard of authority, their failure to recognize God speaking through the leader? But this was a different company altogether, now that the Jordan had been crossed. Joshua's people had given themselves over to God. And although the plan of action was contrary to all human wisdom and judgment, because *God* gave the order there was not a question or a murmur but instant and implicit obedience (6:8-9).

Because of Israel's faith and obedience to God's orders, see what complete victory He gave them. On the seventh day the walls of Jericho fell down flat, the people and animals were killed, and everything was burned. Jericho was utterly destroyed—put out of the way forever.

Now pause and think: Is there some Jericho standing in your way? Is there something in your life that has been one of Satan's strongholds for years? What is it? Some besetting sin, some tendency to evil, some mastering appetite, some deeply rooted habit, some subtle temptation? It must be faced and dealt with. Learn from Joshua's plan. First talk with God. That is the all-important thing—to get the right instructions. Then let all the men of war—all the forces of your being—be directed against this thing, realizing that the Ark of the Covenant, God's own presence in the Person of His Son, is with you. Persistently encompass the thing, then shout out your praise, for God will give you the victory.

Joshua's army was to observe a significant command: They were to destroy everyone in Jericho, except Rahab and her family, and everything except the silver, gold, brass, and iron, which were to go into the treasury of the Lord. No soldier was to take a thing from Jericho to enrich himself. Because the place and everything in it was "accursed" (devoted) to the Lord (v. 17). There were probably many things in the houses of Jericho that the Hebrew soldiers would have liked to keep to beautify their own tents—rugs, pictures, or curious workmanship. But the order was that everything be destroyed. In the next lesson we shall learn that one man disobeyed orders, and we shall see the fearful consequences of this disobedience.

Marla —

Other Notes:

1. The "trumpets of rams' horns" (6:4) were jubilee trumpets usually used only with reference to the religious year of jubilee (Lev. 25). "This suggests that the trumpets carried by the priests had a ceremonial rather than a martial reference. This was a religious, not a military undertaking."[1]

2. "The wall fell down flat" (6:20). "Literally, *the wall fell in its place*, i.e., it collapsed—except for the portion by Rahab's house. Whether an earthquake was used by God or not, it was a miracle of timing and completeness."[2]

3. "Cursed be the man . . . that riseth up and buildeth this city Jericho" (6:26). Refortification was forbidden, but resettlement was allowed (cf. 18:21, a reference to the allotment to Benjamin). Read 1 Kings 16:34 for the exact fulfillment of the curse. "An older view is that Hiel actually offered up his two sons as 'foundation sacrifices.' According to a newer view, the lives of the boys were cut off as a divine visitation upon Hiel for his disobedience in restoring the city God had cursed."[3]

IV. SUMMARY

There is a simple formula to the successes of God's people. Three words tell the story:

Promise *give u Jericho*
Obedience — *marched as told*
Fulfillment — *easy defeat*

As a concluding exercise, show how chapter 6 of Joshua illustrates the formula.

Promise + Obedience = Fulfillment

1. Francis Davidson, ed., *New Bible Commentary* (Grand Rapids: Eerdmans,. 1953), p. 229.
2. Charles F. Pfeiffer and Everett F. Harrison, eds., *The Wycliffe Bible Commentary* (Chicago: Moody, 1962), p. 213.
3. Ibid., p. 330.

Defeat and Victory at Ai

A fter the fall of Jericho, Joshua's fame spread rapidly through the country. The next logical place to attack was Ai, ten miles west of Jericho, commanding a strategic position on the main route from Gilgal to Bethel. Refer to the map on page 36 for the locations of the places cited in this lesson. Ai was a fortified city, smaller than Jericho, having its own king.

Israel had just won a glorious victory over a strong city—Jericho—which we have likened to some large obstacle in our lives. Then the Israelites went up against a smaller city (which we might liken to a "lesser" evil), and they failed. Why? Often one gains the victory over a big besetting sin and yet fails in the matter of some miserable little irritation or impatience, which, in comparison, may seem small but nevertheless hinders one's progress and communion and victory. Study this lesson carefully, and look for many important spiritual lessons.

There are two parts to this lesson (chaps. 7 and 8), and if you so desire you may want to study them separately, in view of the multitude of items recorded in each chapter. Chapter 7 tells of Israel's defeat at Ai, and chapter 8 tells of their subsequent conquest of Ai, after the cause of the defeat was uncovered and dealt with.

Joshua 7

I. ANALYSIS

Read through the chapter at least twice, slowly and carefully. Analyze especially the words of the Lord and the words of Joshua. Use the accompanying chart with its outlines to suggest some of the organization of the chapter. Record your own analytical studies.

Be sure to record key words and phrases of the text inside the paragraph boxes.

JOSHUA 7

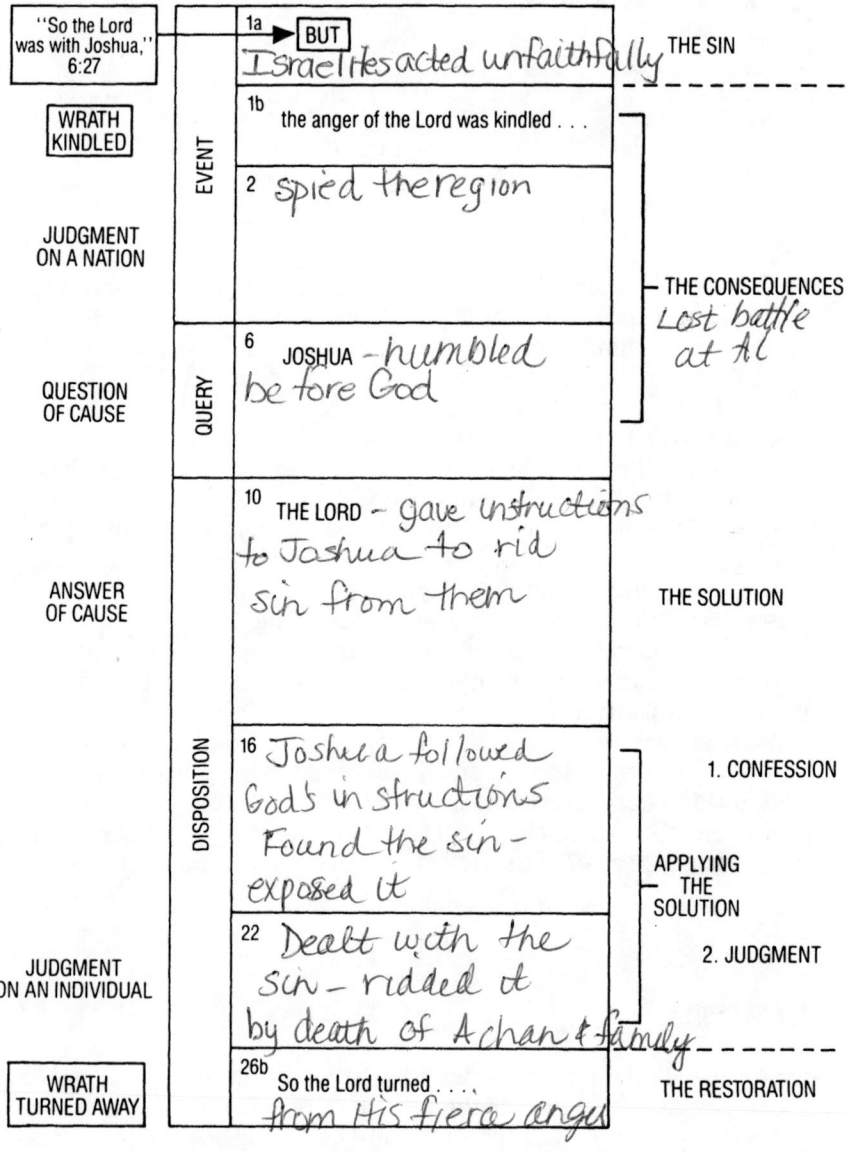

"So the Lord was with Joshua," 6:27		1a **BUT** Israelites acted unfaithfully	THE SIN
WRATH KINDLED	EVENT	1b the anger of the Lord was kindled . . .	
JUDGMENT ON A NATION		2 spied the region	THE CONSEQUENCES Lost battle at Ai
QUESTION OF CAUSE	QUERY	6 JOSHUA – humbled before God	
ANSWER OF CAUSE	DISPOSITION	10 THE LORD – gave instructions to Joshua to rid sin from them	THE SOLUTION
		16 Joshua followed God's instructions Found the sin – exposed it	1. CONFESSION APPLYING THE SOLUTION
JUDGMENT ON AN INDIVIDUAL		22 Dealt with the sin – ridded it by death of Achan & family	2. JUDGMENT
WRATH TURNED AWAY		26b So the Lord turned . . . . from His fierce anger	THE RESTORATION

44

1. Why is 7:1 placed at the beginning of this chapter?

To explain the reason for their lack of success

2. How do you account for Joshua's spies making a critical error in estimating the strength of Ai? (Cf. 7:3 with 8:25.)

only a few men are there - smaller city than Jericho - didn't know about the sin & God's anger

3. What were the effects of Israel's defeat upon the nation and upon Joshua?

the hearts of the people melted, confusion Joshua was mournful & confused, repentant

4. Specifically what was Achan's sin? Why was God's anger kindled before God over this?

He had taken some of the devoted things that were forbidden by God lack of obedience

5. What were the different steps in Achan's sin? How does this illustrate the usual workings of sin? _He coveted,_

He stole, he lied, he hid the goods - (covered up sin) Sin can seem small & insignificant, but it effects many & can cause serious harm

6. Why would all Israel be judged for one man's sin? What does this teach about the fellowship of God's people?

All of Israel had to be committed to conquer the land - Obedience was a must evil could spread

7. Compare "neither will I be with you any more" (7:12) with 6:27.

The Lord was with Joshua & all of Israel, but because of sin - the Lord was not going to be with them unless they got rid of the sin

8. What is involved in the word "except" of 7:12? What does this teach about God? sin

God cannot tolerate sin - He was not going to be with them until they ridded themselves of the sin among them

45

9. What had to be accomplished for restoration of Israel to fellowship with God and power against the foe?

Confession of sin, repentance &
forgiveness   sin had to be destroyed

10. What do you learn about Joshua from his dealings with Achan in verses 19-25?

He was firm & direct, demanded truth,
showed leadership & obedience to God's
command

11. Achan is called Achar in 1 Chronicles 2:7, a name that means "trouble." The name Achor (7:24) also means "trouble." Explain 7:25-26 in the light of this. In what ways and time does sin bring trouble?

Achan brought trouble to his family and all of
Israel, — the Lord brought trouble to him &
family (death)

12. Compare the ending of the chapter with the beginning.

Sin was identified — sin was
punished

13. List the important spiritual lessons you have learned from your study of this chapter.

Take sin seriously, Identify sin &
confess it —

II. COMMENTS

When Joshua and his army prepared to attack Ai they were totally unaware that one of their number had committed a serious trespass and had brought God's judgment upon the entire nation (7:1). We are not told what attitude of heart was the Israelites' when they sent spies to Ai. But the spies made a serious miscalculation of the number of the foe (7:3), which brought on the Israelite's subsequent defeat and devastated morale (7:5).

It is interesting to observe that even the experienced Joshua did not diagnose the defeat correctly. In extreme exasperation, he spoke strong words to God, alternating between questions and exclamations. He overlooked the one thing that always brings defeat: *sin*. When God got Joshua to his feet, He stated the cause clearly: "Israel hath sinned."

God went on to say (7:12-13) that there would be continual defeat unless Israel put away their sin, because He would not be with them unless they did so.

Perhaps the reason that the church is not the power it should be in the world is because so many in the church are living in unconfessed sin. Is there need for stricter discipline in the church? (Cf. 1 Cor. 5.)

There was sin in the camp of Israel, but where? No one but God and the guilty one knew. But inasmuch as the sin of the one affected the whole company and rendered them helpless before their enemies, it had to be searched out without delay and judged. So the next morning the tribes passed one by one before God in review, and Judah was taken. One would least expect to find failure there. Judah was the strongest tribe, leader in the march and in war, and was the tribe through which Christ was to come. Of the families of Judah, the Zarhites were taken; of this family, the household of Zabdi; and of the men of that household, Achan. The fate of Achan (7:24-26) was surely a very needful lesson for Israel. "Whoever touches *hērem* becomes *hērem* and thus devoted to death."[1] (Compare the story of Ananias and Sapphira—Acts 5.)

Let us apply this passage to ourselves. If you and I are not getting the victory over some little town of Ai in our lives, we should not blame God for the failure but bring our whole being before Him and let Him point out our Achan. Let our life pass by in tribes, so to speak. Carefully scrutinize the business life to see if anything there is displeasing to God. Then survey the social life, the home life, the religious, the public, the private life. It may be that we will find the cause of failure where we least expect it. But when we have found our Achan let us not spare him. Stone him to death, burn him, put a heap of stones over him.

Read carefully Achan's confession (7:20-21) and observe, in verse 21, the four downward steps in his sin. "I saw," "coveted," "took," "hid." When we see something God has forbidden, the best thing to do is immediately to turn our eyes and thoughts from it, because, if we continue looking, we will be sure to covet and are likely to take the last steps—"take" and "hide."

Notice again how the truth of the oneness of God's people is taught here. Really only one man, Achan, had disobeyed the command regarding Jericho property, but God said (7:11), "*Israel* hath sinned," "*they* have also transgressed," "*they* have even taken of the accursed thing," "have also stolen, and dissembled," "*they* have put it even among their own stuff." One member of the body

---

1. Charles F. Pfeiffer and Everett F. Harrison, eds., *The Wycliffe Bible Commentary* (Chicago: Moody, 1962), p. 214.

cannot sin without weakening the whole body. One member of the church cannot sin without weakening the whole body of Christ.

The events of this chapter forcefully illustrate some important lessons about sin and its judgment. Let us be stronger Christians for hiding this part of God's Word in our hearts.

Joshua 8

I. ANALYSIS

Chapter 8 tells the story of restoration. Whenever the penalty for sin has been paid, God in His grace restores us.

There are two main parts to the chapter: (1) restored courage (conquest of Ai; 8:1-29) and (2) renewed consecration (altar at Ebal; 8:30-35).

A. Conquest of Ai (8:1-29)

Read through these verses carefully, visualizing the action as you read. Keep in mind the following outline:

(a)	God's encouragement	(8:1-2)
(b)	Test of courage	(8:3-13)
(c)	Courage in battle	(8:14-24)
(d)	The rewards	(8:25-29)

1. Observe the various instructions God gave Joshua (8:1-2). Why does God talk about Jericho at this point? Does God demand faith here, as He did at Jericho?

It's a reminder of their miraculous defeat of Jericho —

2. The strategy of battle against Ai involves decoy and ambush. Does this preclude the miraculous?

no vs. 7 the Lord your God will give it into your hands —

3. Different groups of Joshua's army had different duties to perform. What spiritual truth does this illustrate?

working together brings victory, unity different spiritual gifts - work together

Eph. 4:11

4. Make a list of some important truths taught in these verses.

Do what the Lord has Commanded
Be obedient
Glorify God

B. Altar at Ebal (3:30-35)

The victory at Ai concluded the first campaign (the central campaign) of Joshua against the Canaanites. This is indicated by the fact that Joshua then led all the people of Israel northward to the plain of Shechem surrounded by Mounts Ebal and Gerizim (see map on page 36), in order to carry out the instructions that Moses had given earlier concerning a consecration ceremony.

First compare Joshua 8:31 with Deuteronomy 27:1-26. Moses' instructions called for the building of two stone structures: one, a stele made of large whitewashed stones on which were to be written the words of the law (Deut. 27:2-4, 8); the other, a stone altar for burnt offerings and peace offerings (Deut. 27:6-7).

1. *Stones for an altar* (8:30-31). What two kinds of offerings are cited here? In bringing these offerings to God at this time, what were the Israelites telling God? (Read Lev. 1:4; 7:11-12; Deut. 27:7 for light on the intent of the offerings.)

2. *Stones for the law* (8:32-35). Why was the ceremony of the law significant to the Israelites at this time? What was God trying to impress upon their hearts through the pageantry of the ceremony? It is possible that Deuteronomy 5-26 was part of the reading made at this time. Read this passage. What is the significance of the phrase "the blessings and cursings" (8:34)?

Do not leave this passage without tarrying long over its teaching of the necessity for *altars of consecration* along the Christian pathway. Jesus often brought His disciples "apart" from the multitudes, and from the activities of serving them, in order to be recharged with spiritual energy.

II. COMMENTS

Joshua's victory over Ai was a gift from God. "And the Lord said ... I have given into thy hand the king of Ai, and his people, and his city, and his land" (8:1). (See also 8:18.)

This is an important lesson for us to learn. We do not have in ourselves strength to resist even what we may consider the mildest of Satan's attacks. We need God's counsel and help in every instance. God can enable us to overcome in every situation. And He will do so if we are but true to Him, look to Him for counsel, and implicitly obey Him. But we must give Him glory and acknowledge that it is not ourselves but God who gives us the victory.

After the triumph at Ai, all Israel made the important twenty-to-thirty-mile pilgrimage into the heart of the country to Mount Ebal and Mount Gerizim, two great mountains facing each other in the center of Canaan. The Canaanites do not seem to have made any attempt to molest or detain Israel. Fear had fallen on the inhabitants of the land, and, at least temporarily, "their heart did melt, neither did there remain any more courage in any man," as Rahab had expressed it. The fortress of Shechem, which guarded the entrance to the valley where the Israelites camped at this time, was probably in friendly hands.[2]

Arriving at Ebal, Israel officially took possession of the land *for God.* Note the proceedings. First they erected an altar and offered burnt offerings and peace offerings to the Lord. Next they set up great stones, plastered them, and wrote upon them the law, probably including the Ten Commandments. Then the tribes arranged themselves on the two mountains according to the instructions given by Moses, six over against Ebal for cursing, and six over against Gerizim for blessing, while the Ark of God, the priests, and Joshua stood between. Joshua read aloud the law of Moses in the audience of the assembled nation—men, women, and children; and all the people said, "Amen."

This ceremony was a highlight of Israel's possession of Canaan. Moses had emphatically commanded it before his death. It was acknowledging God and His law in the center of the country and proclaiming allegiance to the King in whose name they claimed the land. They had written the law of their King in the heart of their country. Even so we have the law of our King written in our hearts. Should we not acknowledge and publicly proclaim our allegiance to Him, offering our burnt offerings and our peace offerings?

When the religious ceremony was over, Israel no doubt returned to Gilgal, which was to serve as the base for their military operations in the next (southern) campaign.

III. SUMMARY OF THE LESSON

As a summary exercise, write out a paragraph telling the story of these two chapters centered on the four words:

2. See ibid., p. 215, for an explanation.

Trespass
Judgment
Grace
Altar

These words form a cycle that was an oft recurring experience in the history of Israel, especially during the years of the judges and kingdoms. Recall Israel's experiences before entering Canaan to see illustrations of the cycle then.

Lesson 7

Remaining Conquests

Joshua's first campaign battles were few but crucial for both Israel and the enemy Canaanites. The battles of this central campaign were crucial because (1) as tests for Israel they demonstrated for all subsequent battles where Israel's true strength lay; and (2) as signs to the Canaanites they confirmed God's continued favor upon Israel.

Before reading these chapters of the southern and northern campaigns, review the survey outline of Joshua 6-12 given in Lesson 5. Part of that outline is shown here:

PACT with GIBEON 9:1	5 KINGS SLAIN 10:1	OTHER CONQUESTS 10:28	NORTHERN CONQUESTS 11:1	"So Joshua took all that land" 11:16 12:24
SOUTHERN CAMPAIGN			NOTHERN CAMPAIGN	SUMMARY

If you have not already done so, record the divisions of this outline in your Bible.

First read through these four chapters in one sitting, underlining key words and phrases in your Bible. During this reading you may also want to identify the geographical locations, with the help of a good map, as they are cited in the narrative. It will add much enjoyment to your study if you visualize the settings in this way. (If you do not check the geography during this first reading, be sure to do this later.)

What are your impressions after reading this? How prominent does the narrative represent God's help to be?

I. ANALYSIS

Now let us study each part separately, looking more closely at the text.

A. Pact with Gibeon (9:1-27)

Read through the chapter carefully and record your observations. Let the following questions suggest some studies:

1. Why did the kings of 9:1 decide to fight against Israel? What military advantage did they count on (9:2)?

They had heard of the Israelites victories over other cities
they joined together to fight

2. Why did the Gibeonites, identified as Hivites in 9:7, want to get under the protecting cover of Israel (9:24)?

They knew they would be killed

3. Read Deuteronomy 20:10-15 as background explaining why the Gibeonites claimed to be foreigners. Also read Deuteronomy 20:16-19 to understand the Gibeonites' words of 9:24.

4. What big mistake did Joshua and the men of Israel make that kept them from recognizing the Gibeonites' deceit?

9:14 They did not inquire of the Lord

5. Why did the princes of Israel insist on keeping the pact that had been made with the Gibeonites (9:19-21)? Read Ezekiel 17:12-19 and 2 Samuel 21:1-6 concerning oaths.

An oath was a very serious promise & could not be broken w/o serious consequences

6. One of the main reasons for God's judgment of death upon the Canaanites was to protect the Israelites from the idolatrous influences of those nations. What then was the problem with sparing the Gibeonites? How was this at least partially solved in Joshua's "curse" upon them (9:23, 27)?

they were left & could influence the Israelites w/ idolatry & evil —
The curse left them in lowly jobs & without power & influence

7. In later years blessing came to the Gibeonites (e.g., in their privilege to help rebuild the walls of Jerusalem—Neh. 7:25; cf. also references to the exaltation of the place Gibeon: Josh. 10:7-15; 1 Kings 3:5-15; 1 Chron. 2:29; 2 Chron. 1:3.) How do you explain the blessing, in view of the curse decreed by Joshua?

B. Five Kings Slain (10:1-27)

1. Locate on a map the cities of the five kings and also the city of Gibeon. Why did the kings want to battle Gibeon?

important city, royal city, larger than Ai men were good fighters

2. Was this the first coalition of armies Joshua had to face? What would have been his normal human reaction? Compare God's assurances given to him then with those given on earlier occasions.

no, panic, fear Do not be afraid of them - I have given them into your hand - no one will be

able to withstand you

3. Two miracles involving nature are recorded here: hailstones, and the sun and moon. How does the last phrase of verse 13 indicate that Joshua's prayer concerning the sun and moon was for military advantage?

It stopped until the nation avenged itself on its enemies

4. Because of different possible readings of verses 12 and 13, authorities differ over their interpretations as to what was the nature of Joshua's request. Each of the following interpretations holds that, whatever happened, the phenomenon was miraculous:

(a) While the battle was proceeding during the early hours of dawn, Joshua prayed for an extension of semidarkness, which God sent by way of the storm of hailstones, lasting throughout the day.

(b) Joshua needed an extension of *daylight* to complete the battle, so he asked for a prolonged day. This God gave by slowing down the earth's rotation, making one full rotation to last forty-eight hours.

(c) Joshua's exhausted army needed relief from the heat of the sun, so Joshua prayed that the sun would "leave off," or become impotent, in its beating down upon the troops. God did this by the hailstorm.

5. Have you ever heard this objection to praying: "Why pray—the Lord will accomplish His will anyway"? How does the phrase of 10:14 "the Lord hearkened unto *the voice of a man*" answer such an objection?

God listened & responded

6. Notice the last phrase of 10:14. How is this an all-inclusive commentary on Israel's battles against the Canaanites?

C. Other Conquests (10:28-43)

1. Locate the places on a map.
2. What are the repeated words and phrases of this section? What is taught by these?

took city, put to sword, totally destroyed
no survivors

3. Notice the all-inclusiveness of the terms of verses 40-43. This paragraph is a summary of the southern campaign.

D. Northern Campaign (11:1-15)

Relatively few verses are devoted to this important campaign of Israel. Much land was involved, but the Israelites needed only to engage in battle in the northernmost parts of Canaan. Again, as you study these verses locate the places on a map.

1. What was the military strength of the kings of the northern alliance? Had Joshua met such strength before?

large number of horses & chariots
huge army (numerous as sand on seashore)

2. As far as military strategy was concerned, what move by Joshua defeated the foe? What assurance had God given Joshua?

hamstring their horses, burn their chariots

3. What spiritual lesson may be learned from 11:15?

leave nothing undone that the Lord commands

E. Summary (11:16–12:24)

Since the battle against the northern alliance was over, it could be said that for all practical purposes Joshua had taken "the whole land" (11:23).

Here and there were still enemies that would have to be routed by the individual tribes when they settled in their territories. At this point, however, the backbone of the Canaanites had been broken, so that the distribution of the inheritances could by accomplished (11:23).

The book of Joshua appropriately records, in summary fashion, the dimensions of Israel's military campaigns. (Study this section of Joshua with the following outline in mind.)

1. Summary of the campaigns
   Geography (11:16-17)
   Duration of battle (11:18) (The "long time" was about seven years.)
   Extent (11:19-20)
   Special mission (11:21-22) Notice the concluding statement of the above summary (11:23).
2. Summary of the Kings smitten
   Kings of Transjordan (12:1-6)
   Kings west of the Jordan (12:7-24)

Before reading the Comments section, write down the various spiritual lessons you have learned from these chapters of Joshua.

II. COMMENTS

A. Pact with Gibeon

Although the various nations of Canaan were usually at war among themselves, when Israel invaded the country the nations became throughly alarmed and united to meet a common foe. They had heard of the unparalleled successes in battle that Israel had enjoyed since leaving Egypt. Their only hope was that although Israel could defeat a single army, they would fall before an alliance.

Evidently the inhabitants of Gibeon had no faith in this alliance and preferred to attempt a league with Israel. They were familiar with God's command to Moses regarding them (9:24). So if they expected to effect a league, they had to conceal the fact that they belonged to these seven condemned nations that Joshua was to destroy. Accordingly, they dressed messengers to look as if they had come from a great distance. One day, entering the Israelite camp near by, they told a most plausible story (9:8-13).

Joshua and the elders were thrown completely off guard. Notice with what apparent reverence the men spoke of Israel's God (9:9) and how careful they were, in speaking of the wonders God had wrought, not to mention the crossing of the Jordan or the fall of Jericho. These had occurred so recently that it was unlikely that the report could have reached a "far country" (from which they professed to have come) before they had left.

Joshua and the elders, although at first a little in doubt, seemed to consider this too obvious a matter to consult God about. Surely they were to use their own common sense and decide some things themselves. So they may have reasoned. We read that they "asked not counsel at the mouth of the Lord, and Joshua made peace with them, and made a league with them" (vv. 14-15).

Israel had yet to learn, as each one of us must learn, that we cannot trust our own judgment or wisdom, any more than we can trust our own strength. Everything must be referred to God. He is our wisdom as well as our strength. This wounds our pride, but it is necessary for victory.

After three days the people found out what a blunder they had made and what a tangle they were in. These pious-talking, innocent-appearing strangers, they found, were their near neighbors—some of those desperately wicked people whom God had commanded should be utterly destroyed. But the oath had already been made "by the Lord God of Israel" that these Gibeonites should live. The matter was patched up as well as possible. Because of the oath, and the Name in which it had been given, the Gibeonites were not killed but were made hewers of wood and drawers of water, thus actually becoming helpers in the service of the Tabernacle.

The personal application and instruction of all this is plain. The condemned nations of Canaan typify the Christian's spiritual enemies of various kinds. We have already studied about great Jericho and little Ai. Now, in this section, the Gibeonites represent not the open attacks but the *wiles* of the devil. These enemies are not less deadly because they use deceit and guile instead of open assault. Indeed, they are far more dangerous because they are not so easily recognized as enemies. Only God's eye can penetrate their disguise and reveal their character. If Israel had consulted God before making any agreement with them, all would have been well.

It is always folly for God's people to make alliances with the enemies of God. How often we see Christians marrying unsaved people or entering into business partnership with the ungodly, as though there were no such command from the Lord as "Be not unequally yoked together with unbelievers" (2 Cor.6:14). We are surrounded by "Gibeonites," enemies of God who, disguised and under assumed friendliness, or in the name of religion, desire to make a league with us. Let us learn the lesson of this story before entering into any league—marriage, business partnership, or social agreement. No matter how much we trust the individuals, or however right it may all appear to us, let us not fail to ask counsel of the Lord.

B. Five Kings Slain

Five kings of the south, infuriated upon learning that Gibeon had joined with Israel, determined to destroy the traitors, and for this purpose they attacked their city. The Gibeonites sent to Joshua a frantic message for help. Joshua, having entered into a league with the Gibeonites, was by honor bound to defend them. Moreover, at the same time he perceived that this was an opportunity to conquer the whole south section of Canaan at one blow. So with all his fighting force he started out from Gilgal, God's assurance of success ringing in his ears, marched to Gibeon, and surprised the combined forces of the enemy by a sudden attack.

Notice how the narrative hardly recognizes the Israelites' part in this battle. God was the Warrior. Joshua tells us that God "discomfited" them, and "slew" them, and "chased" them, and "smote" them. And as the nations were fleeing before Israel, a terrific hailstorm burst upon them, as though the whole artillery of heaven had suddenly opened fire. And more died from the hailstones than from the sword.

As Joshua saw how the Lord was fighting for them, his faith rose, and he made this remarkable prayer: "Then spake Joshua to the Lord . . . and he said in the sight of Israel, Sun, stand thou still upon Gibeon; and thou, Moon, in the valley of Ajalon" (10:12). Someone has amplified this prayer thus: "Why should not the sun, which is Thy creature, but worshiped too long in this land in Thy stead, now subserve Thy purpose in the destruction of these who have given it what was Thy due? And why should not yonder moon, which has so often looked down upon these licentious orgies of the Amorites, now see their impurity washed out by blood? They are Thine, Jehovah; they will perform Thy bidding; harken to my voice and let them stay."

And the Lord harkened to Joshua, "and the sun stood still, and the moon stayed, until the people had avenged themselves upon their enemies" (10:13).

This stupendous miracle continued for about a whole day. What a testimony this was to the almighty power of the God of Israel. Like the miracles in Egypt, this should have been sufficient to convince the Canaanites that the things they had been worshiping were nothing and that the Lord was the only true and living God. How fitting it was that the sun and moon, which in this land had been worshiped in place in God, should be thus invoked to the assistance of Israel and as absolutely subject to the living God.

C. Other Conquests

After that great day, on which God had given such an astonishing display of divine power on behalf of His people, Joshua went from city to city, conquering as he went, until the whole south of Canaan was subdued and taken.

Read carefully 10:28-39, and you will see that seven cities were destroyed. Joshua was careful to carry out the Lord's instructions (see 10:40), and the reason for this tremendous victory was "because the Lord God of Israel fought for Israel" (10:42). With grateful, rejoicing hearts the army must have returned to the camp in Gilgal (10:43) and told the women and old men and boys and girls of the wondrous things that their God had done for them in the war.

D. Northern Campaign

Joshua and his army had just returned from the conquest of the southern section of Canaan when they heard of a vast coalition against them in the north. Jabin, king of Hazor, hearing of all that had taken place in the south, summoned to his aid the kings of the north and west, and their united armies pitched at Lake Merom, some distance north of the Sea of Galilee, prepared to fight with Israel. How foolish of them to think they could fight successfully against God. They knew that God was with Israel. They had heard of Him and His power, as had Rahab. If, like Rahab, they had believed in God, and taken their stand with Him, they too could have been saved. But like Pharaoh before them, they sinned against the light they had been given, their hearts hardened, and they refused to yield.

When Joshua heard of this impressive grouping of armies —hosts of armed men, horses, and chariots at Merom—he was not daunted but immediately set out with his army to meet the foe. Upon arriving in the vicinity of Merom he was probably tempted to be dismayed at the formidable array of the enemy. But God reassured him with the promise "Be not afraid because of them: for tomorrow about this time will I deliver them up all slain before Israel" (11:6).

Have you noticed that the Lord, in promising victory, always emphasized "*I* will"? Never for a moment was Israel allowed to suppose that the victory had been won by their own strength. It was God who conquered the enemy and presented the land to Israel.

This was one of the greatest battles of Joshua's career. The enemy was completely routed, and the cities were destroyed. But although the strength of the foe was broken, Joshua carried on war with the individual kings for several years, as we read in 11:18: "Joshua made war a long time with all those kings." This evidently refers to different parts of Palestine and to different kings.

III. CONCLUSION

One part of Joshua's work, the conquest of Canaan, was complete. But a large part still remained to be performed. He had been commanded not only to bring the people into the land and subdue it but also to settle them in their new home. The next two lessons concern the division of the land among the tribes, according to the word that God had spoken by Moses in Numbers (26:52-56).

Lesson 8

Special Allotments

The second half of Joshua records the not-so-active engagements of Israel's allocation and appeal, whereas the first half of the book has much action.

1	13	22 24
ACTION	ALLOCATION	APPEAL

Chapter 13 begins the third main section of the book of Joshua, The Inheritances. Recall from the survey studied in Lesson 1 that the book of Joshua is divided into four main parts:

1	6	13	22 24
PREPARATION	CONQUESTS	INHERITANCES	CONSECRATION

Why not review the survey study you made in Lesson 1 before you go any further in your analysis of the next chapters of Joshua. It is always helpful in Bible analysis to keep the overall view in focus.

The Inheritances: (13:1–21:45)

One more brief survey should be made—this one of the section Inheritances (chaps. 13-21). Using the accompanying chart as a guide, glance through these chapters, making a mental note of any prominent things observed along the way.

JUDAH	SONS OF JOSEPH	7 TRIBES

(handwritten diagonal notes along the chart:) 13:1 Still areas of land to be taken over · 13:8 their land East of Jordan River · was given by Moses · given Hebron · 14:1 · 15:1 · 16:1 · 17:1 · 18:1 · 19:1 · 20:1 · 21:1 · 21:43

INTRODUCTION	2½ TRIBES	CALEB	9½ TRIBES	LEVI	CON-CLUSION
SPECIAL ALLOTMENTS			MAJOR ALLOTMENTS	SPECIAL PROVISIONS	
Lesson 8			Lesson 9		

Feel free to make any notations in your Bible or on the accompanying chart, as you do this survey reading. Notice which chapters are studied in Lessons 8 and 9, respectively.

Special Allotments: (13:1–14:15)

I. ANALYSIS

A. Introduction (13:1-7)

Where does the first command appear in this paragraph?

vs 6 Be sure to allocate this land to Israel for an

(Note that verse 7 is included in the first paragraph.) What is the reason for recording what precedes it?

This unconquered land was part of their inheritance & God wanted them to

Read 1:6 again to see what duty Joshua had been instructed to perform regarding the inheritances. From 24:29 we learn that Joshua died at the age of 110. The phrase of 13:1 probably refers to an age between 90 and 100.

continue to conquer it

inheritance

62

The areas still containing many enemies are cited in verses 2 to 6. The general locations were in the southwest and the far north. Locate the places on a map. Why would God allow His people to settle in the land when there were still enemies to be disposed of? What spiritual lessons may be learned from this?

He wanted them to remain faithful

We must face challenges & stay faithful

B. Special Concession (13:8-33)

The allocation of these lands to the two and one-half tribes had already been made by Moses (Num. 32). God's words to Joshua end with verse 7; the remainder of the chapter is supplied to make the record of allocations complete. *The Wycliffe Bible Commentary* suggests that verse 8 be read thus: "With him (i.e., with the other half-tribe of Manasseh) the Reubenites and the Gadites had received their inheritance." In your reading you will also want to substitute "had" for "have" in verses 15, 24 and 29. (Note: Read Num. 32 if you are not familiar with the story of how these tribes received the trans-Jordanic land for their inheritance.)

Compare the "inheritance" of verse 32 with the "not any inheritance" of verse 33. What was to be the Levites' *real* inheritance? What do you learn from this? (Note: The Levites were to be given cities according to chap. 21, but these were not considered land inheritance.)

Their inheritance was to serve God, not care for property & ~~farm~~ land. Their needs were provided for by God & gifts from the people they served. — We should care for the missionaries & pastors that teach & serve God

C. Special Reward to Caleb (14:1-15)

The first paragraph (14:1-5) of chapter 14 introduces all the succeeding sections that record the allocations of land on the western side of the Jordan. What does the paragraph indicate as to who of-

The Red Tent

ficiated in the task, and the method used? Refer to a commentary for a description of the procedure of lot.

Analyze carefully verses 6-15. You will find many blessed spiritual truths in these lines—and between the lines. What kind of a man was Caleb? What did he mean by "I wholly followed the Lord my God"? (v. 8). Describe such a walk for a Christian. Be sure to write out a list of the various truths taught by these verses.

II. COMMENTS

When God called to Joshua and spoke to him the words of 13:1-7, Joshua's work as a warrior was over, but he had much to accomplish now as a statesman. His was the important and delicate task to inspire the nine and one-half tribes (1) to accept wholeheartedly and without complaint the territories that the lots would determine to be theirs, (2) to take up residence in the land without unnecessary delay, and (3) to rout any enemies still lingering in the land.

Although Israel had a right to the land in one sense, they did not have the land in another sense. It had been conquered in general, but it also had to be conquered in detail. To illustrate: The first settlers in America conquered the land when New England was settled, but there was a great deal of conquering done afterwards. Each man fought for his own piece of ground—drove out the wild beasts, felled the trees, ploughed the ground, and held it against the enemy. In the same way, although Canaan was conquered by Joshua in the general sense of the word, it was still necessary that each tribe take its special portion of the land and with God's help subdue it completely.

But we notice—looking ahead in Joshua's account—that the individual tribes were not keen on cleaning out the land, for personal ease and apathy soon began to supersede zeal for God (see 13:13; 16:10; 17:12; and 18:3).

The church should learn an important lesson on witnessing from this failure of Israel. Our great Joshua, Christ, met and conquered all the assembled hosts of Satan and won back from him the dominion of this world. In the beginning, God gave man dominion over the earth, but man, by taking orders from Satan rather than from God, handed over that dominion to Satan. Christ later spoke of him as the prince of this world. Christ came to slay this evil one by dying on the cross. When He so conquered, He ascended to His Father and sat down at the Father's right hand, surveying the vast domain that He had taken. Then, sending the Holy Spirit to empower His disciples, He put into the hands of the church the work of conquering the world in detail, of bringing into subjection to Him the individual inhabitants of the world. But how faithful has the church been in fulfilling its mission? Surely now, as ever, "there remaineth very much land to be possessed," and our great Joshua has need to say unto us:

"How long are ye slack to go to possess the land, which the Lord God of your fathers hath given you?" (18:3).

But there was one in the company of Israel who was not slack. He stands as a model for every soldier of the cross—sturdy, lionhearted Caleb, whose enviable record is that he "wholly followed the Lord." As the tribes assembled at Gilgal to receive by lot their inheritance, Judah was the first to receive. But before the lot was taken, Caleb, now a white-haired old man, stepped forward. He reminded Joshua how, more than forty years earlier, when the two had returned to Kadesh-barnea with the ten unfaithful spies and had given their report, God had promised land to Caleb. No doubt through all those years of wandering this promise had gladdened Caleb's heart. His eye was set on Hebron. Hebron had been the home of the fathers of their nation, Abraham, Isaac, and Jacob; and at Hebron these old patriarchs, with their wives, lay buried.

The difficulties in the way of possessing Hebron and the great fenced cities held by the giant Anakim were not insurmountable in Caleb's eyes. He simply said in his great faith:

"If so be the Lord will be with me, then I shall be able to drive them out, as the Lord said" (14:12).

How uncommonly fine that is. Such faith is never unrewarded, and in 15:14 we see how he drove out the giants. Caleb's great faith and strength and loyalty to God enabled him not only to obtain for himself but to give to others, as in the case of his daughter Achsah, to whom he gave the upper and the nether springs, in addition to the wedding dowry of a field (15:16-19). Later also Caleb unselfishly yielded his city, Hebron, to the Levites, content to dwell in the suburbs (21:12).

III. A CONCLUDING THOUGHT

As you conclude this lesson, why not let the words of this challenge "Give me this mountain" (14:12) ring in your heart. Determine, with the help of the Lord, to live in the place of God's will for you, even though giant enemies threaten.

Major Allotments and Special Provisions

Many golden nuggets of truth can be found in these chapters by looking beyond the long geographic sections. Actually, a study of the geography itself can be gratifying. This would be a good time to make a tour of Palestine. Secure a good map of the land, showing the boundaries of the tribes, and follow the descriptions of the borders and cities as Joshua records them. A commentary will help identify some of the more difficult locations. *The Moody Atlas of Bible Lands,* by Barry J. Beitzel, is highly recommended.

I. ANALYSIS

In your analysis, look for repeated words and phrases; important conjunctions, such as "but" and "yet"; and any comments, actions, or conversation recorded from time to time. It will not be difficult for you to catch the special notes Joshua records in the descriptions.

A. Major Allotments (15:1–19:49*a*)

(Note: Let 19:49*a* read, "So they made an end of distributing the land for inheritance by the borders thereof," ASV).

1. *Judah* (15:1-63). Observe that the borders are described in 15:2ff., and the cities are listed in 15:21ff. Watch for this outline in other chapters. What does 15:13-19 reveal about problems of occupation? Concerning the problem of verse 63, recall from chapter 10 that Joshua did not capture Jerusalem in the battle of the southern campaign. What spiritual truth does this illustrate?

2. *Sons of Joseph* (Ephraim and Manasseh (16:1–17:18). What verses contain "but" and "yet"? Study carefully the paragraph

17:14-18. What do you learn here about complaining, pride, work, faith, and true strength? Analyze especially verse 18.

We must be willing to work for our needs. Don't be afraid to do what God has asked us. Have faith that God will help us.

3. *Seven remaining tribes* (18:1–19:51). Judah, Ephraim, and Manasseh, the more prominent of the tribes, were given the largest and most valuable lands of Canaan. That distribution was made at Gilgal (14:6). Apparently the other seven tribes were given the responsibility of initiating the allocation proceedings for their people, for they were rebuked by Joshua for their laxity in doing so (18:3). Observe the setting of 18:1. Locate Shiloh ("rest") on a map. Concerning the procedure of allocation, it appears that the size and strength of each tribe determined the value of the parcel received, whereas the drawing of lots determined the geographical location assigned. Observe that the lots were cast "before the Lord our God" (18:6)—emphasizing what?

that the Lord determined the places— reminding them that God was in control

Now that you have read the text recording the allocations of the land, look at a map of Canaan and study the general locations of the tribes. Keep in mind the various advantages of location that any tribe would normally hope to receive, such as arable land, walled cities, size of territory, water supply, roads, neighboring lands, and so forth. Do you see any case where a tribe might have reasoned that its allocation was not adequate? Why was it so important, therefore, that the procedure of lots was used in the allocations?

Simeon ↑ Zebulun was surrounded (no access to Sea or Jordan River - this procedure eliminated conflict or favoritism & allowed God to be in control

Consider the sovereign purposes of God in what He gives His people today. Some Christians are given large responsibilities; others are given smaller ones. Some are called to one type of ministry; others to a different kind. Try to think of the various things that make Christians as different one from the other as the lands of the tribes differed, in terms of what God gives. Read 1 Corinthians 12 for further light on this matter.

God gives gifts of wisdom, knowledge, faith, healing, miraculous powers, prophecy, administration, speaking in tongues, interpret tongues

After you have studied the subject of the previous paragraph, consider this question: What one basic spiritual requirement did God expect of each tribe, irrespective of its location or size? What does God require of you, in your service for Him? (Cf. 1 Cor. 4:2; Matt. 25:14-30). In view of all this, what are your thoughts on fame and fortune?

Obedience

For help in seeing some of God's purposes fulfilled even in the land distributions of the tribes, consult a commentary (e.g., *The Wycliffe Bible Commentary*, pp. 226-27).

B. Special Reward to Joshua (19:49*b*-51)

Observe the brevity of this reference and the smallness of Joshua's request. Timnath-serah was a city on the bleak north side of the mountain of Gaash (Judg. 2:9). What does this teach you?

C. Special Provisions (20:1–21:42)

The six cities of refuge (chap. 20) and the forty-eight cities of dwelling for the Levites (chap. 21) were God's provision for certain needs of the people. Study these chapters with this thought in mind, and try to determine what spiritual lessons are illustrated here.

D. Conclusion (21:43-45)

The concluding paragraph of this section is a key paragraph in the book of Joshua. Analyze it carefully, observing the many things taught. (As shown in earlier lessons, *all* the enemies were not yet routed. To learn God's purposes here, read Ex. 23:29-30 and Deut. 7:22-24.)

II. COMMENTS

The setting up of the Tabernacle at Shiloh was of great significance to Israel at this time. (Cf. Acts 7:44-45; Jer. 7:12.) Geographically Shiloh was about in the center of Canaan. In our study of the book of Numbers we saw that the Tabernacle always occupied a central position among the tribes, whether Israel was on the march or in camp; and once Israel was settled in their homeland, the Tabernacle, God's dwelling place, was located in the center, as He Himself would be at the center of His people's life—their national life, their religious life, their social life, and their home life. The Tabernacle remained in Shiloh during the entire period of the judges (the Ark was removed in the time of Eli—1 Sam. 4:4).

If every tribe had been as faithful and diligent as was Caleb, they soon should have driven out all the enemies and possessed all the land according to God's ideal for them. But they were not like Caleb. They were content to let large portions of their inheritance remain entirely unexplored or remain in the hands of their enemies. In this respect are we not much like them? We do not possess even half of all that God has for us in Christ. (Read Paul's prayer for the Ephesian church, Eph. 1:15-23.)

The children of Joseph were dissatisfied with the portion assigned them (17:14-18). They said they wanted more territory because they were a great people; the land that had been given them was not sufficient to contain them because of all the forested hills. Joshua then challenged, "If you're so great, cut down the forests yourself and make more room." And when the people still complained, Joshua resorted to encouragement, "Thou art a great people ... for it is a wood, and thou shalt cut it down ... thou shalt drive out the Canaanites" (17:17-18).

Many Christians, like the children of Joseph, ask for larger places of usefulness, while they are failing to use the opportunities actually within their reach. I once taught Bible classes in a town in a Western state. A young woman seemed intensely interested in the study of the Bible. She told me how she longed to work for God. Her great ambition was to go to the foreign mission field, but the way had not been opened, and she could not at all understand why. She was eager and willing to serve God in a large way, but it seemed that she was not allowed to do so.

One day I had occasion to call at her home, and it was then that I sensed what was wrong. She had need of just such an answer as Joshua gave the children of Joseph. There was much work for God to be done in the place she now occupied—her own home and neighborhood—but as far as I could learn from herself and others, she had never even made an attempt in that direction. Although she was sighing to win to Christ the heathen in far-off lands, she had never tried to win her little brothers and sisters to Him. Nor had she even brought them to Sunday school, or read Bible stories to them, or taught them verses of Scripture. Before we conclude that we are such a great people that we need to inherit more than one portion, let us look around and see if there remains any unoccupied territory within the limits of the portion already assigned to us.

One or two things of importance must be noted before we conclude this lesson. One is the appointing of the six cities of refuge about which God had instructed Moses. Three were on the east side of Jordan and three on the west. The three on the east were Bezer, Ramoth, and Golan. The three cities of refuge on the west were Kedesh, Shechem, and Hebron. Locate these on a map. Notice by their relative locations that a manslayer in any of the tribes would have fair access to refuge from the avenger of the blood he shed. Thus we see that provision was made in the land of promise for the passing over even of the sin of taking human life, provided it was not done in presumption and did not emanate from malice. How much more gracious is the refuge in the shadow of the cross, where redemption is offered for *all* sins.

The forty-eight cities were given by the tribes to the Levites in accordance with God's instructions delivered to Moses (Num. 35:1-5). In these cities the Levites lived while they were not working about the Tabernacle, and there were the homes of their wives and children. Each of the twelve tribes gave some cities, so that the Levites would dwell in all parts of Israel, permeating the land with the sacred influence of Shiloh. The Levites taught the law of God, looked after the purity of the neighborhood, discerned between clean and unclean food, and acted as judges in matters of controversy.

"And the Lord gave unto Israel all the land which He sware to give unto their fathers; and they possessed it, and dwelt therein. There failed not aught of any good thing which the Lord had spoken unto the house of Israel; all came to pass" (21:43, 45). If we turn back to Exodus 6:6-8 and observe the seven "I wills" that God had promised to the children of Israel before they left Egypt, we learn something of the faithfulness of God. The promises were given to an oppressed nation living under the bitter bondage of Pharaoh. Only by the miraculous and gracious hand of God could such a people be delivered and brought into a prosperous land, a land of rest for their souls and fellowship with their God.

What encouragement here for the sinner. When a poor wretch, under the bitter bondage of Satan, deep in sin and ignorance and degradation, hears God's wonderful promises, it often seems to him incredible that God could give him the peace, joy, power, and fellowship that he sees some saint enjoying. But if the wretched, downtrodden one will only put his hand in God's, and follow where He leads, he will see all this accomplished, and even more. He will find himself, one day, without spot or wrinkle, presented faultless before the throne of His glory, conformed to the image of God's dear Son. Is anything too hard for God?

III. SUMMARY

> These are the inheritances, which
> Eleazar the priest, and
> Joshua the son of Nun, and
> the heads of the fathers of the tribes of the children of Israel divided for an inheritance
>> by lot
>> in Shiloh
>> before the Lord,
>> at the door or the tabernacle of the congregation.
> *So they made an end of dividing the country* (19:51).

As you conclude your study of this lesson, tarry over this summary verse, and see how many truths each phrase teaches.

Lesson 10

Altar of Witness

Chapter 22 begins the fourth and last major section of Joshua, entitled "The Consecration."

1	6	13	22 24
PREPARATION	CONQUESTS	INHERITANCES	CONSECRATION

As of this time in Israel's life, the land had been divided among the tribes, and the people were beginning to enjoy the blessings of God's rest land (21:43-45). At the beginning of such an important era it was fitting and necessary for the Israelites to consecrate themselves to the Lord, vowing to be obedient and faithful in the days and years to come. This is mainly the subject of the last chapters of Joshua. The chapter studied in this lesson concerns the two-and-a-half eastern tribes—Reuben, Gad, and Manasseh.

I. ANALYSIS

Read through the chapter carefully, with pencil in hand, making notations as you read. Decide for yourself how the chapter follows an outline. You should have no difficulty in doing this. You may want to make an analytical chart of this chapter. The following questions will guide you in your study.

73

1. From this chapter alone, how do you know that the hearts of both the western and eastern tribes were right with God at this time?

They had carried out - obeyed all that God Moses & Joshua had commanded - God gave them rest

2. Compare the atmosphere of the opening paragraph (vv. 1-6) with that of the closing paragraph (vv. 30-34).

They had obeyed & were returning to their land for rest -

They were faithful - the Lord was w/ them

3. Read 22:1-8. Make a study of the indicative and imperative verbs of verses 2-5:

> *Indicative*
> Ye have . . .   (2-3)
> The Lord hath . . .   (4)
> *Imperative*
> Return ye . .   (4)
>   etc.   (4-5)

Make a special study of the six commands of verse 5. How do these apply to Christian living today? Why were the tribes given the rewards of verse 8?

love the lord your God, walk in all His ways obey His commands, Hold fast to Him, Serve Him with all your heart & all your soul, This is exactly how we are to live.

This was part of the blessings God gave them

4. Read 22:9-29. What kind of altar did the eastern tribes erect? (Compare v. 34; Ed means "witness.") What was their motive? Why were the western tribes alarmed over the project? What is the strength of the word "beside" in verse 19? Compare the eastern tribes' altar with the altar of the central sanctuary prescribed in Deuteronomy 12:13-14.

an imposing altar - motive was as a memorial, a witness between them and the rest of the Israelites and the generations to follow

They thought they were breaking faith w/ God and worshipping idols

Deut - was an altar in a place the Lord chose

5. Read 22:30-34. What do these verses teach about reconciliation and unity within the fellowship of God's people?

They met & discussed the problem—did not just act & react—
They restored fellowship by communication

6. Write out a list of some of the valuable spiritual lessons to be learned from this chapter.

Love the Lord your God
Walk in His ways
Obey His commands
Communication solves problems

II. COMMENTS

It is interesting to observe that the six commands of Joshua recorded in verse 5 have mostly to do with the *walk* of the believer, whereas the action of the rest of the chapter has mostly to do with *worship* (involving the altar). One thing we may learn from this is the intimate relationship of the believer's walk and worship.

Although it is true that the western tribes misunderstood the motives of their brethren east of the Jordan, they may be commended for their intense concern lest anything mar the fellowship between Israel and God. They did not quickly forget what had happened because of Achan's sin.

Nothing in this chapter indicates that the eastern tribes sinned in the motives of their project. In fact the last verse emphasizes the commendable testimony of these people concerning their God. At the same time it may be fair to say that they were shortsighted in their knowledge of God's provisions for unity among the tribes, for Israel's thrice-yearly gathering at Shiloh's altar (Ex. 23:17) was to have helped keep the tribes bound together.

One more comment: Joshua's charge (v. 5) to these people was to *keep on* walking in God's ways. It was not long before their commendable testimony (v. 34) became a thing of the past and apostasy set in, as we see from the people's refusal to come to Deborah's aid in fighting some enemy Canaanites (Judg. 5:15*b*-17*a*).

III. CONCLUSION

Israel's experience in connection with the altar of Ed gave further assurance of God's fellowship with them: "This day we perceive that the Lord is among us" (22:31). In many different ways Israel was learning the importance of this intimate relationship: *Immanuel*—"God with us." Would that they had retained this conviction in later years.

Christians can enjoy the full blessings of "rest land living" only as such a fellowship is maintained: "Truly our fellowship is with the Father, and with his Son Jesus Christ. And these things write we unto you, that your joy may be full" (1 John 1:3-4).

Lesson 11

Renewal of the Covenant

Probably nearly twenty years elapsed between the end of the war and Joshua's death, during which Israel had been quietly dwelling in the land, cultivating and enjoying it. But they evidently had made no attempt to drive the Canaanites completely out of the country, as God had instructed. Before long Israel found to their sorrow that these enemies, that had been allowed to live as a smoldering fire, were eventually breaking out in unquenchable fury.

Joshua, whose influence had kept Israel loyal to God, was about to leave them. As Moses did just before his death, Joshua called all Israel to him to hear his parting words of warning and challenge.

I. ANALYSIS

These two chapters contain two main parts: Charge given (chap. 23) and covenant renewed (24:1-28). The last verses (24:29-33) form a fitting conclusion to the book by recording the death of Joshua and other concluding items. In this lesson you will concentrate on the two units named above. Read each unit carefully and prayerfully, applying the Word to your own circumstances as you study.

A. Charge Given (23:1-16)

1. How much reference does Joshua make to himself? How would

Faithful heart _worryed about his family_

you describe his heart in this farewell address? In what ways does he exalt God?

I am old & well advanced in years (I have allotted as an inheritance for your tribes all the land of the nations that remain, nations I conquered) _God speaking_
He gives God much credit & glory

2. Analyze the commands and warnings of this chapter. Apply the truths to present-day Christian living.

We must obey God's word, not put our pleasures & plans ahead of God's, Love the Lord our God

3. Analyze how Joshua sets forth the "law of recompense" in verses 15-16. Try to recall some New Testament passages that teach this law.

obey - rewards
disobey - punishment

B. Covenant Renewed (24:1-28)

All the events of this segment lead up to the covenant of verse 25. Actually the experience was a renewal of the covenant relationship that God had originally established with His people through Abraham. Before proceeding with your analysis of this segment, review Israel's history prior to this event as it had reference to the covenant. (A concordance will locate the passages of Scripture written in the earlier books about the covenant.)

1. Why do you suppose Joshua gathered all the tribes to Shechem? (For help in answering this, read Gen. 12:6-7; 33:20; 35:1-4; Josh. 8:30-35.) _foreign idols buried there_
It is where God made the promise to Abraham to give this land to his offspring 1st altar

2. What was Joshua's purpose in giving a résumé of Israel's history? (24:2-13).

It was a reminder of all God had done for them - He wanted them to remain faithful & not fall back into old sins.

78

They threw away foreign gods

3. Tarry long over verses 14 and 15. What many truths do you learn here?

We must decide whether to obey the Lord or not. — We must serve Him with all sincerity & truth

4. Read 24:16-24. Why did not Joshua quickly accept Israel's commitment? What eventually convinced him that the people were in earnest?

He knew they made promises before & broke them — They reviewed all that God had done for them —

5. How would the actions of verses 25-26 serve to help the Israelites?

The covenant, the stone & the recorded laws of God would remind them of who they serve & promises made to follow God

C. Death of Joshua (24:29-33)

These verses center on Joshua, Joseph, and Eleazar. Study them carefully to learn the many blessed truths taught here.

II. COMMENTS

Joshua's farewell address, in outline and plan, is much the same as Moses'. He first reminded Israel of all that God had done for them in the past; he called attention to their present favored condition; and then he faithfully showed them what would be the consequences if they continued to obey God, and what would be the consequences if they forsook Him and worshiped idols.

Joshua's chief anxiety was regarding the enemies that still remained in Canaan. He urged Israel to drive them out altogether. Although he himself had to leave the people, he pointed them to their true Leader, God (23:5). He warned them of the danger of having anything whatever to do with the Canaanites. They were not to visit them, or intermarry with them, or even mention the names of their gods. They were to love and serve Jehovah and be courageous to do all that was written in the book of the law, not turning to the right hand or the left. If they should fail to do this, then, just as truly as God had fulfilled His promise regarding the good things, so He would keep His word and bring upon them all the evil that He had said He would for turning from Him.

This was all for the good of Israel. If they could but be induced to follow God, He would lead them to glory; but if they should follow Satan, he would lead them to destruction. Joshua, as the mouthpiece of God, rehearsed the history of Israel from Abraham down, and as his hearers thought over these things they must have been persuaded that the God who had never failed in the past would never fail in the future.

Joshua called upon them to come to some decision then and there—to make up their minds once for all whether they would serve God or not. This was their hour of decision. Joshua was clear as to what he would do: "As for me and my house, we will serve the Lord" (24:15). Eventually Joshua was able to lead his people to the same commitment to the Lord. It was only then that he would "let the people depart, every man unto his inheritance" (24:28).

Joshua's influence was so great that even after his death, throughout the days of the elders who outlived him, Israel continued to serve the Lord. No better word could be written concerning the influence of a believer's life upon others.

III. SUMMARY OF THE BOOK OF JOSHUA

The study of a book of the Bible is never complete without reviewing the entire book after one has completed his study.

Make this your concluding study. See how much of the survey chart you can remember. Going on from here, make a summary list of the main truths taught by this book of the Bible. You may want to break down this list into groups, such as:

Truths about God
Truths about victorious living
Truths about blessing and judgment
Truths about the Word

Now that you have studied Joshua for yourself, why not plan some ways in which you can share its blessings with others? Faithful Bible study leads to communication:

1. Observation
2. Interpretation
3. Application
4. Communication

Remember, faithful Bible study helps you learn and experience truth. This should lead to communicating truth—sharing it with others.

God's truths never fail

As for me & my 80 *house, we will serve the Lord —*

Bibliography

RESOURCES FOR FURTHER STUDY

Archer, Gleason L. *A Survey of Old Testament Introduction*. Chicago: Moody, 1964.
Jensen, Irving L. *Jensen's Survey of the Old Testament*. Chicago: Moody, 1978.
The New International Version Study Bible. Grand Rapids: Zondervan, 1985.
Payne, J. Barton. *An Outline of Hebrew History*. Grand Rapids: Zondervan, 1970.
Pfeiffer, Charles F., and Howard F. Vos. *The Wycliffe Historical Geography of Bible Lands*. Chicago: Moody, 1967.
The Ryrie Study Bible. Chicago: Moody, 1978.
Strong, James. *The Exhaustive Concordance of the Bible*. New York: Abingdon, 1890.
Tenney, Merrill C., ed. *The Zondervan Pictorial Bible Dictionary*. Grand Rapids: Zondervan, 1963.
Unger, Merrill F., ed. *The New Unger's Bible Dictionary*. Chicago: Moody, 1988.
Wood, Leon. *A Survey of Hebrew History*. Grand Rapids: Zondervan, 1970.

COMMENTARIES AND TOPICAL STUDIES

Blaikie, William G. *The Book of Joshua*. Minneapolis: Klock and Klock, 1978.
Blair, Hugh J. "Joshua." In *The New Bible Commentary*, ed. F. Davidson. Grand Rapids: Eerdmans, 1953.
Bush, George. *Joshua and Judges*. Minneapolis: Klock and Klock, 1981.

Hamlin, E. John. *Inheriting the Land: A Commentary on the Book of Joshua.* Grand Rapids: Eerdmans, 1983.

Jensen, Irving L. *Joshua: Rest-Land Won.* Everyman's Bible Commentary. Chicago: Moody, 1966.

Pink, Arthur W. *Gleanings in Joshua.* Chicago: Moody, 1964.

Rea, John. "Joshua." In *The Wycliffe Bible Commentary*, ed. Charles F. Pfeiffer and Everett F. Harrison. Chicago: Moody, 1962.

Sanders, J. Oswald. *Promised Land Living.* Chicago: Moody, 1984.

9 780802 444707